T0113563

AVENUES
TO
SUCCESS

An Entrepreneurial Highway

PAUL PENTZ

authorHOUSE®

AuthorHouse™
1663 Liberty Drive
Bloomington, IN 47403
www.authorhouse.com
Phone: 833-262-8899

© *2020 Paul Pentz. All rights reserved.*

No part of this book may be reproduced, stored in a retrieval system, or transmitted by any means without the written permission of the author.

Published by AuthorHouse 08/11/2020

ISBN: 978-1-7283-6939-6 (sc)
ISBN: 978-1-7283-6938-9 (e)

Library of Congress Control Number: 2020914485

Print information available on the last page.

Any people depicted in stock imagery provided by Getty Images are models, and such images are being used for illustrative purposes only.
Certain stock imagery © Getty Images.

This book is printed on acid-free paper.

Because of the dynamic nature of the Internet, any web addresses or links contained in this book may have changed since publication and may no longer be valid. The views expressed in this work are solely those of the author and do not necessarily reflect the views of the publisher, and the publisher hereby disclaims any responsibility for them.

CONTENTS

Foreword vii

Chapter One 1
Chapter Two 11
Chapter Three 18
Chapter Four 28
Chapter Five 43
Chapter Six 53
Chapter Seven 64
Chapter Eight 73
Chapter Nine 82

FOREWORD

"An entrepreneur is a person who organizes and manages a business or industrial undertaking. An entrepreneur takes the risk of not making a profit and gets the profit when there is one." (World Book Dictionary)

Obviously not all entrepreneurs succeed. This is particularly true in restaurateurs. When entrepreneurs are successful the rewards may be great, including wealth, independence, and personal satisfaction, among other things.

Living in a high-end golf community following retirement, I have had the opportunity to meet numerous highly successful entrepreneurs. I admired their independence and I often wondered whether there were common personality characteristics that led to their successes. Perhaps there were common circumstances that fostered success. The more I discussed backgrounds with these people the more interested I became.

I decided to write this book with a chapter devoted to each of numerous entrepreneurs to see if I could find the common building blocks that pave the "Avenue to Success". The objective of this book is to demonstrate to the intended entrepreneur the struggles, the failures, the grit, the courage, and the determination that one must have to go it alone. For that is what an entrepreneur does. He or she makes the decisions, accepts the consequences of those decisions, and reaps the rewards or suffers the losses. They risk their own money, time, and heartache, seeking not only wealth, but personal achievement, and occupational independence.

Obviously, in a community like this I did not meet the entrepreneurs that failed. This book is not dealing with failure. It is intended to foster success. In these chapters you will find some individuals that did fail along the way, but who had the determination to pick up the pieces and start again. You will find a variety of interesting backgrounds and circumstances that often made the hope of future success very doubtful. These individuals rose above that. They took chances, they spent time, they risked money, they sacrificed personal relationships, and they won.

In the concluding chapter I will try to pull together the common threads of these individuals. Their years of success have given them the opportunity to look back and thoughtfully reflect on what made them successful.

May the lessons found in this book help to lead you to your own future success!

CHAPTER ONE

"You can't climb the ladder of success with cold feet."
Author unknown

HONESTY, COURAGE, AMBITION

Hub Labels, Inc.
Bud Dahbura

Born in Bethlehem, Palestine in 1932 Abbud "Bud" Dahbura is a vibrant, effervescent and jovial man who has enjoyed great success in business, in love, and in friendships. He is the owner of Hub Labels, Inc., a flourishing business that produces printed labels for a multitude of products found on today's retail shelves. He has been happily married to Mary for Fifty four years. And he is a friend to everyone he meets. What more could anyone want?

Bud grew up in Bethlehem which he describes as beautiful with flowers everywhere, wonderful fruits and fresh water springs in many places. " It is a lovely place to live." He had four brothers and one sister. His father's first marriage ended with the death of his wife and two of his four children to cholera. Bud's father avoided the dread disease as he had been in Central America at the time seeking opportunities for wealth for the family. Upon return by steamship he found his wife and two children and many of his friends and relatives had been taken by the cholera epidemic. Keep in mind that travel in the early 1900s was not a matter of jumping on a Pan Am flight. It was a long, arduous journey.

At an advanced age, probably 58, Bud's father remarried to a twenty four year old woman and sired six more children, one of which died at birth. Bud was the youngest in the family having been conceived when his father was already 68 years old.

Being elderly, Bud's father no longer worked but he did invest in a fabric and clothing business which his oldest son George ran. With seven people in the family and only one working, it was a real struggle to put food on the table. George sacrificed his own higher education to run the business and earn money to support the family. It was important to him that his brothers have an opportunity for higher education. Even without college, George too was very accomplished. At one time he went to Cyprus and worked for BBC. Concentrating on taking care of the family George didn't marry until he was fifty.

Palestine was a British Colony at the time, therefore, even though Arabic was the primary language, it was required that starting with third grade everyone learn to speak English.

Growing up was a struggle. Putting food on the table to feed everyone was a challenge for brother George but he did it. Then the war years came and there was fighting in the streets of Bethlehem. At times Bud went to school, lying face down on the floor of the school bus to avoid the possibility of being hit by gunfire. "It was terrible; there were bombs and bullets everywhere." Eventually it got so dangerous that the large regional schools were closed and children went to small local schools for instruction in limited subjects. These small schools had about twenty students each but were safer than the big schools and the necessary transportation to get to them.

Brother Anton was the second eldest and he chose to go to medical school at The University of Cairo in Egypt, apparently taking long train rides from Jerusalem to Cairo across the desert. He too succeeded, eventually ending up as a physician in Baltimore, Maryland.

At twenty one years of age Bud wrote to the University of Texas requesting admission and financial support. Fortunately, he received a full scholarship and set off for the states. What a big and courageous decision in the life of a young man to leave his country and his family. He did it. His college expenses were about $30 per year. It wasn't easy though as he needed money for housing and food. In addition to the regular studies in mechanical engineering Bud, as a foreign student, was required to take American history courses.

Working three separate jobs in addition to going to school Bud was able to earn enough money to get by. He lived in a rented apartment with a number of Middle Eastern students who were all a bit homesick. Bud wrote to his mother for recipes for eastern food and, to the delight of his friends, became a very good Middle Eastern chef.

"Any job that came along was worth doing. I worked hard but I loved it. We had fun and I had an opportunity to get ahead." If one thinks about the environment in which Bud grew up, it is easy to see the built in work ethic that was likely the foundation for his eventual success.

While at the University of Texas, Bud asked one of his professors if he could help get his brother Anton, the doctor, to the states to further his education in the medical field. This effort enabled Anton to come to Elizabeth, New Jersey for an internship and then to Baltimore, Maryland for his residency. He eventually became a very successful physician in Baltimore.

Upon Bud's graduation from the University, there was no thought of going on for a master's degree. Earning a living was the most important thing on Bud's mind. With his brother Anton now living in Baltimore, Bud chose to move there and to try to find a job as a mechanical engineer for any company. It was a start.

Bud's first job as a mechanical engineer was with Ellicott Machine Company which specialized in dredging equipment. His attention was evidently diverted by Mary, a lovely young nursing student. According to Mary, "Bud never took long to make up his mind, on their first date he talked about when they were married". She thought "who is this man"?

Mary was originally from Hagerstown, Maryland and following graduation from nursing school chose to go home and start her career there. A lovesick Bud visited on the weekends for about a year and then they got married. One weekend while they were dating, Mary had to work so Bud took her mother for a long drive in the country. He came upon Landis Machine and Tool Company in Waynesboro,

Pennsylvania and filed an application for a job for which was accepted.

Mary and Bud got married in 1959 and went on a one week honeymoon to New York before starting his new job. On the first day of work, Bud went to the head of the company and said I have no money, can you give me an advance so that we can eat. He got the advance and proved to be a very valuable and grateful employee.

After three years Bud was recruited away by Pangborn Corporation, a manufacturer of grinding machinery and sand blasting equipment. To this day Pangborn is still using a number of Bud's designs for machinery.

By 1967 Bud and Mary already had two children, Tony and Tami. Older step brother Ernesto in El Salvador kept encouraging Bud to come to that country where the economy was booming and there were many opportunities to make money. Ernesto wisely insisted that Bud was too smart to be working for someone else and should be running his own business.

Without a job, but in possession of hope, self-confidence, and the lure of family, Bud, Mary and the children (Tony 7 and Tami 5) set out for El Salvador. He looked for something to make, rejecting many ideas, until he found a roll of scotch tape in a store and asked who makes this down here. The answer – no one. He wrote to 3M and they were not interested in manufacturing in that small of a market so Bud took it on himself. His brothers helped to finance the venture and Bud began importing giant rolls of adhesive tapes, cutting them into small retail packages and selling them to corporate and retail outlets. This included

5

cellophane tape, electrical tape, duct tape, etc. The business was a big success.

Bud imported the large rolls of tape from Tuck Tape in the United States and from Sellotape in England. Sello was his favorite for quality, service and price. He basically had no competition in the Central America market. His success soon attracted the interest of 3M who made an insufficient offer to buy him out.

Always looking for new opportunities Bud became interested in making printed pressure sensitive labels and he learned to print on flexographic equipment. Thus he introduced pressure sensitive labels to Central America.

Originally Bud and Mary had agreed to stay in El Salvador for only five years; however, at the end of the first five years Bud sold the printing and tape business but suggested they stay on for another five. He had another idea. He decided to make thread cones for the storage of thread. He bought the equipment from Japan and had it installed by some Japanese workers who spoke no English. He worked with them through interpreters. Another successful venture!

Probably the most fun business they developed in El Salvador was the introduction of Hardee's Hamburgers to Central America. Bud was able to secure the franchise for Hardee's for all of Central America and proceeded to open seven restaurants, four in San Salvador, two in Guatemala and one in Costa Rica. The restaurants were so successful that they created traffic jams in the streets in front of them. As an innovator Bud would stage television sets on the stores patios for the patrons to watch broadcast fights which brought big crowds and lots of sales. Even the president of Hardee's came down at one point to marvel at their success.

As a side note, Bud tells of attending a business speech where the presenter ended by pointing at a young man sitting in the audience and ordering him to stand up. The young man cautiously stood and was told to look under his chair. There he found a one dollar bill taped to his seat. The presenter said "See you can't make a dollar unless you get off of your ass." End of speech! Perhaps that is a lesson for all of us.

In 1967, having spent ten years in El Salvador the Dahburas were becoming increasingly nervous as civil war was threatening the safety of their family. They sold the businesses and planned to return to Hagerstown, Maryland. Bud contacted his old company, Pangborn who was so eager to get him back that they paid all expenses for the family to come home. Bud resumed his engineering career, the kids went to school and Mary settled for the now less exciting life of being a stay at home housewife.

Once again the idea machine kicked in and Bud told Mary he had an idea for a business she could run. He would start making pressure sensitive labels and she could run the business. They called it Hub Labels. The name came from the fact that Hagerstown was often referred to as the hub of commerce in that area.

Starting with a typewriter, a metal desk, a secretarial chair and a four drawer metal file cabinet (three drawers were empty) they started a business which is now the largest pressure sensitive label business under one roof east of the Mississippi River.

Mary started with the Yellow Pages and a dial telephone soliciting business. One of her first good customers was the local Wonder Bread Bakery who bought small circular labels that said "Buy one get one free" and pricing labels.

At first they rented a store front with 20,000 square feet. They had one press, a table model, and one converter. After six months they moved to a larger facility that they bought and then in another six months they added on to it.

Growth came from word of mouth. The majority of the business was from local customers. Eventually they attended printer's shows, at one of which, they met a broker who helped put their name in the marketplace.

For four years Bud continued to work his day job, went to the production facility after work and printed labels until midnight or even two A.M. In the morning Mary would go to the office, pack up the labels and deliver them. Never afraid of hard work they kept this pace until they were successful enough for Bud to leave Pangborn and work full time at Hub Labels. The largest order they ever received to this day was from the United States Post office for nearly five hundred million small labels with an S printed on them.

Quoting Bud, "You do what you've got to do to be successful. Sometimes lack of sleep, long hours, and personal sacrifice make the difference between success and failure."

Today Hub Labels employs about 150 people, down from the peak of just over 200, through some careful weeding by their son, Thomas. Thomas runs the company today bringing to the table a business degree in economics and finance. He continues the same ethical and moral policies as Bud and has brought strong growth to the business. Thomas is married and has one daughter, Wren.

There have been two union attempts, both of which have failed. Said Bud, "It's pretty simple, pay a fair wage, offer good benefits, communicate thoroughly, and keep an open door to everyone and you won't have a union." "We have physical fitness programs, smoking cessation programs, health programs, weight watchers, all of which we pay for." "We care about our people." And obviously they care about Bud and Mary.

Hub Labels has grown over the years to a one hundred and ten thousand square foot operation producing between twenty and thirty million labels per month. When asked what were the keys to this tremendous success he said "honesty is the key, never cheat anyone, be faithful, give good advice, build relationships, don't be greedy, honesty pays". "One must be a risk taker and must be sufficiently committed that when things are not going well to make them go well. Work hard!" Proudly, an aging Bud tells of the many phone calls he continues to receive from long- time customers to wish him well.

Discussing the hurdles he has faced, Bud states that competition has been very tough. Today the competition from China is very difficult to deal with. Another disappointment or perhaps a challenge is the focus of big businesses on price. "Everything is price, not safety, not service, not even quality, just price."

On what made Bud succeed he again says "honesty". "Say it like it is. Tell it like it is". "Don't try to squeeze every dollar out of every transaction, be fair and honest with everyone."

Today Bud divides his time between Hagerstown and Naples, Florida. He loves golf, fine dining, and friendships. His enthusiastic personality, positive attitude, and strong laugh are a magnet for everyone he meets.

When in Hagerstown Bud still goes to the coffee shop at six A.M every day for breakfast with the supervisors. That keeps him focused on the issues at hand and keeps the supervisors in touch with his feelings. He maintains an open door policy so that anyone can walk into his office at any time if they need to speak with him. He pays well, gives good benefits, and cares about his employees. "I'm proud that my employees frequently bring their children to meet and play with me. I give them candy."

I guess Mary sums it up well with a final statement "It was not easy but in all honesty, we had a good time".

CHAPTER TWO

"Progress always involves risk; you can't steal
second base and keep your foot on first."
Frederick Wilcox

WORK, SACRIFICE, WORK

Encore Commercial Products
Ron Klein

My father, Sam Klein, had a shoe fetish. He always wore the most expensive shoes. Most likely it was because when he was a child he had to put cardboard in his shoes to protect his feet.

Dad quit school in the eighth grade to sell newspapers on the street in Detroit. He made that extra effort to make a few dollars. He always wanted to do all he could do to help support his family.

Dad went on to work in a factory and later as a produce buyer for a supermarket chain. Mom, Helene, was a stay at home mom which was characteristic of families in those years. We were a one car family so when dad was at work we were without transportation. As a produce buyer, he worked from very early in the morning until early afternoon. Dad always provided for us as well as he could, and we considered ourselves middle class. I'm not sure that we were, but at least that is what we thought of ourselves.

Dad was only about 5'8" tall and not very large. Amusingly, his job in the factory was on the production line where he had to hoist some heavy parts and move them from one conveyor to another. He worked alongside the world champion boxer, Joe Lewis, whose job was to count the parts that dad moved. Joe was on the company boxing team so he didn't have to do any heavy work. Dad soon decided to join the boxing team so that he might get a better job but boxing didn't turn out to be a good idea.

Ron, born in 1942, was the eldest of three children, including a brother and a sister. He states clearly that his father's work ethic has been a driving force in his own life.

As a child, Ron attended public school where he was anything but a scholar. He enjoyed the fun parts of school rather than the studies. When he graduated from high school he went on to Ferris Institute, in Big Rapids, Michigan, (now Ferris University). After one year Ron transferred to Wayne State University where he claims to have majored in political science and gin rummy. Again, he enjoyed the fun times more than the academics. He spent two years there but did not graduate. "In that time, I thought if I could only make $15,000 per year I would be set for life." How financial times have changed and how they will change in the future is anyone's guess.

During the summers, while in college, Ron and a friend drove to The Catskill Mountains, near Monticello, New York, where he found work as a waiter. He progressed in the second summer to become a maître d', where he worked for the next three years. Wow, his first tuxedo!

A year later Ron went back to Detroit where he landed a job as the Manager of the Main Dining Room at the Pontchartrain Hotel. "One of the things that I learned from my hotel experience was the art of selling. When one can convince an unhappy dining customer to come back and try another meal, a real sales job has been accomplished."

During those two years at the hotel Ron met his future wife, Lin Magy. Now it was time for a real career move. Lin had been brought up just a few blocks from Ron in a similar social setting. They had not met earlier because she was in a different school system.

Ron's first career effort was selling computer and office supplies in 1967. This of course was at the very beginning of the age of computers. At that time, computers printed, using large ribbons, similar to typewriter ribbons. Today, our young people don't even know what a typewriter, or a typewriter ribbon is. It delivered the ink to the paper when the letter keys were pounded. Ron worked for a base salary plus a commission.

Ron tells of a friend in the business who happened to be calling on Chrysler when their computer ribbon broke. He offered a sample that he had in his brief case, thereby solving a big problem for Chrysler. For that he earned their loyalty and business for quite some time. There is a lot to be said for being in the right place at the right time. One must get out and make the calls and sooner or later the effort will pay off. The harder you work, the luckier you get.

Ron married Lin in 1967 and he began a new career selling Group Insurance for Blue Cross/Blue Shield. We had a Ford Custom 500 as a family car. At that time, servicing the car was more like check the gas and fill up the oil. I had many opportunities for a job at that time, but Blue Cross offered a company car which I could not resist. I worked there about twelve years with a new car provided every two years. I was allowed to pay a little extra to get air conditioning in the car which reduced my dry-cleaning bills and certainly improved my appearance on sales calls. I sold group health insurance for a salary plus bonus.

At Blue Cross promotions were mostly title rather than functional. At one time, I was offered a sales training position wherein I would train others and receive raises based upon their increases in productivity. I was interested but turned it down as I wanted to be in control of my own destiny through my own sales efforts.

The first business that I owned was a partnership with Frank Spodafore. Frank had been a friend and associate at Blue Cross. Frank had some college and he and his wife became our best friends as well as my business partner.

We started our own business, Midwest Benefits Corporation, which was housed in a larger agency. Our business was selling group life and health insurance policies. We sought clients through prior contacts and cold calls. We specialized in $500 deductible and $1,000 family deductible policies that ultimately evolved into one of the largest third-party administrators in the country administering self- insured medical plans. In the early 1980s interest rates exploded into the high teens which helped drive our business. We were small at first but eventually built the business to more than 200 employees and a very sizeable and successful business.

In 1990 there started to be talk about a potential "Hillary-care" when Bill Clinton became President of the United States. This could potentially devastate our business. We received a good offer from FFMC, First Financial Monetary Company, so we sold the business with a multi-year performance contract, and a non-compete agreement, for the two of us. We continued to build the business but found that being somewhat out of real authority didn't appeal to us. We then renegotiated our contract and got out.

At that time Frank's wife became ill and passed away after about a year. Fortunately, the sale of our business allowed Frank to devote a full year to enjoying life with his wife before she passed.

With a new partner, Bruce Liebowitz, we then bought into a Pharmacy Benefit Management company, Claimspro, that was basically a prescription drug claim processing business. We successfully built this business up over a ten-year period. Basically, we gave our clients a great deal. We didn't take rebates from pharmaceutical companies so we were able to offer the lowest prices of our competitors. We simply charged one dollar for each prescription that we processed. Perhaps we could have made more money if we accepted those rebates but we were just driven to provide the lowest cost to our customers. We just didn't know any other way to do business. Anyway, we built up the business and after ten years sold it in the year 2000 to CVS Pharmacy.

At 64, I was too young to retire so my partner and I started looking into property management. We felt that if we could buy some shopping centers or strip centers we could manage them for a good return. The problem was that anything worth looking at was sold to the bigger hitters in the industry and we only had options on the dregs. Forget that idea.

My partner, Bruce, and I then met a fellow, Stuart Bernstein, in Michigan, who had an idea for bollard covers. Bollards are steel posts that protect drive up banking windows or toll booths, or gas pumps, etc. from errant cars. These posts historically get banged up frequently which results in unsightly rusty polls and significant maintenance cost. The idea was to make an inexpensive, colored plastic cover for the polls that can be replaced periodically at minimal cost.

We formed a company called Encore Commercial Products to produce the bollard covers. "Stuart had the idea for us but not the finances nor the management skills to develop the business. Based on Stuart's information we were led to believe that ninety percent of the polls were the same size. This meant that we only had to invest in one mold to support ninety percent of the potential business. Molds were a significant investment. Perhaps we should have studied the business more but impulsively we jumped in.

We quickly learned that not only were there different heights to the polls but also different widths. This meant a very large investment in molds which fortunately we could afford. Bruce and I did not take any money out of the business until it got on its feet, otherwise it likely would not have survived. To be successful, businesses must have staying power.

We invested in utilizing something called blow molding which gave us the opportunity to make covers at a much faster pace and at a lower cost of approximately thirty dollars versus competitive rates of about sixty dollars. Our business grew mostly through trade shows, parking lot service companies, distributors, and the internet.

Stuart passed away after a couple of years, from a blood clot, following back surgery.

Our business has grown to what is now probably the largest or the second largest of its kind in the United States. We don't manufacture anything, we outsource the manufacturing. Today, we have twenty-five employees in Michigan, a sales office in Toledo with three people, and a subsidiary in Ontario, Canada. We still own the business and I remain somewhat active with a few phone calls each day. Basically, it is run by Bruce and a few key employees.

When asked why Ron always had a partner in each of his businesses he said the following. Having a partner that you can trust allows you to get away without fearing that the business will go downhill. Also, having a partner that will tell you when an idea or a decision is wrong is worth a lot. I learned early on that I could feel awfully smart with everyone who worked for me agreeing with my thoughts until I got home and found that I was always wrong.

When asked to what Ron attributes his success he said I go back to my father's training, when he told me to always do what it takes, be willing to make the extra effort, and be willing to sacrifice personal time, comfort, and security to be successful. One must be willing to take risks. I believe in the philosophy of the turtle, if you do not stick out your neck you can never get ahead. Successful careers are quite often being in the right place at the right time, having the vision to see opportunities, and having the courage to act.

CHAPTER THREE

"The people who get on in this world are the people who get up and look for the circumstances they want, and, if they can't find them, make them."
George Bernard Shaw

HOME BUILDER
PATSY CARTER RATTIGAN

In Maysville, Oklahoma, a town of fifteen hundred, I, Patsy Hoffman, grew up on a small dairy farm. My mother milked the cows, I strained and bottled the milk, and then I delivered it to homes in the morning and evening. I did this until I was fifteen. At the same time, mom worked as a waitress and I went to school. We had very little and we worked hard for everything that we did have. Eventually dad got a job as chief of police and we moved to town. I was so glad to get off of the farm.

Dad liked to buy and sell houses and was able to make enough money for the family in that manner. Each week he gave me $1.25 for school lunches which, at that time, cost $.25 per day. I didn't tell him, but I took a job in the school cafeteria for free lunch so I was able to save the money. One part of my household duties was to make all of my own clothes. The money simply was not there for us to go shopping for clothes. In the summers and after school I picked cotton which had to be the worst job that I ever had.

Our family consisted of my parents, a sister Betty, ten years my senior, and a sister Linda, two years my elder. Actually, Linda was my cousin but her mother left her with us at an early age. After a number of years, when Linda's mother returned, my mother went to court to ensure that Linda would remain part of our family and under mother's custody.

In high school, I played on the girls' basketball team, ran track, and was a pitcher on the girl's soft-ball team. I was a good student and had a very small scholarship to college from competition in the Junior Miss Pageant, but we simply did not have the money for me to go to college.

Probably the most influential person in my life was Peggy Hanson. She was the wife of Pat Hanson who ran the bank in Maysville. They had a wonderful large house with all of the accoutrements. I babysat for the Hanson's children and even occasionally traveled with them as a sitter. That was the first time that I ever slept in a hotel. I was so new to it that when I got up in the morning I made my own bed, not knowing that hotels have maid service. Wow! This was really living.

Peggy often took me shopping and gave me lots of clothes. Through her, I saw what the good life could be. I was motivated to secure a life of wealth and class. I knew I would not find that in Maysville and just wanted to get out of there. The heck with picking cotton, I wanted the good life.

Upon high school graduation, at the age of eighteen, I married my high school sweetheart, Rick Burgess, who was a star football player. He had a scholarship to Oklahoma State. Through some unfortunate judgement the coach took a number of freshmen recruits to Mexico for a "fun time". The end result was that my husband, and others, and probably the coach, were dropped from Oklahoma State and Rick ended up at Wichita State. While at Wichita I worked for Scholfield Pontiac as a credit manager, to support the two of us.

The biggest disappointment in my life was that due to some health conditions, I was unable to have children. My first husband, Rick, wanted so much to have his own children that we divorced after seven years of marriage. We're still friends but it was necessary for us to go our separate ways.

Following our divorce, I moved to Dallas to look for a career. I knew only one person in Dallas, Jody Ferrer. Jody and her husband Chuck invited me to live with them and gave me a job as secretary for one of their businesses. They owned Executive Suites which was basically a floor in one of the high rises which was divided into about twenty to twenty-two individual units for small business offices. I acted as a switchboard operator for all of the sublets and did other secretarial duties as needed.

In high school, I took three bookkeeping courses, and through a government program for low income people, I was fortunate to have been given a job working for the school secretary. I also was able to type at a rate of 120 words per minute. These classes, typing skills, and the secretarial exposure gave me sufficient background for Jodie to employ me to do the bookkeeping, write leases, and do other secretarial chores for the organization and its tenants.

Eventually they expanded to seven different Executive Suite businesses. I worked for them at several different times over the years. Eventually, I functioned as General Manager for all of them, supervising thirty-five women in various parts of town.

In 1976 I met Coy Carter, fifteen years my senior, with two sons, Craig and Ken. We married in 1978, and I, at the young age of twenty-seven had a family of my own with two teenage boys. Ken was in college and Craig came to live with us for a short time.

Coy was a marketing genius. He worked for Oklahoma National Life Insurance Company, which dealt with insurance policies written at the time that a car was purchased from a dealer. Coy's responsibility was to train the finance and insurance representatives that worked for car dealerships. Because of the frequent turnover of personnel at car dealerships, and the opening of new dealerships, Coy was constantly on the road, training new people. This also involved a number of relocations for us. Eventually, we were transferred back to Dallas. I, once again, went back to work for Jody in the Executive Suites business. Coy was headed out of town one day and called me to say that he wanted to quit his job and start his own extended warrantee business.

We had just bought our first house and had used all of our savings to do so. Coy said, if you support me for a few years, when this business gets going, then you can start your own business in whatever you want to do. Coy founded United American Warrantee Limited. It was a struggle, but we did it. I worked for Jodie, went home after work, and spent each evening preparing solicitation letters for the warrantee business.

In the early stages, Coy did his business through car dealerships. It was slow going. At that time car dealerships offered 12,000-mile one-year warrantees. Coy's idea was to offer 24,000-mile two-year warrantees. We bought a huge automatic typewriter that had the ability to personalize each letter that we mailed. We never did telephone solicitation but we sent out lots of letter solicitations. The response was fantastic. Money poured in like you would not believe. So much so that it required that I leave my job and work full time with Coy to build the business, to process claims, and to manage the reserve accounts.

We had checked with the state insurance authorities and found that we were not considered an insurance company so we did not fall under their supervision. We were however, personally determined to build capital reserves so that we could always cover every claim. So much money came in that we started opening accounts at many different banks because the banking guarantees were limited for only the first $100,000 of deposits. As it was, we built up nearly $5,000,000 in reserves.

Having achieved success and security, Coy said, now it is your turn. You have always been interested in selling houses, why don't you build some houses?

Knowing nothing about building houses, I needed quite an education. This was really a long shot. We contacted Gary Robertson, the construction supervisor that worked for the contractor that had built our own house. We paid Gary $5,000 to let me spend every day with him to take notes and to learn from watching and listening to him. I guess you would call this a crash apprenticeship. I met him six days a week at 6:30 AM and ended each day at 7:00 PM. We inspected plumbing connections before the slabs were poured, we supervised the pouring of the slabs, we left no stone unturned. I took careful notes on everything that he did as well as to follow the sub-contractors to ask questions about what they were doing. Finally, after seven months, I was sufficiently confident that I could start out on my own. I founded Regency Homes LLC., and went to work.

Successful building is mainly about the quality of your sub-contractors. Being a female in a "man's world" was not easy. I knew of only one other female builder but she was over in Arlington, Texas. I was in Dallas. I never met her.

Fortunately, most of the sub-contractors knew me from my time learning from Gary. It did not take long for me to gain their confidence. I made sure that I tracked them down every Friday to give them their paycheck. Builders are notorious for slow pay to the sub-contractors, so I was well received. There was never any question about them getting paid. They learned to trust me.

I only built speculative homes, never a home for a client. I did not want the pressure of working with the whims and indecisions of people building their own castles. Between 1983 and 1998, through the ups and downs of the economy, I built forty-two houses in the Dallas area and sold them all. Now we had two successful businesses running in our small family.

In a surprising, and disappointing turn of events, the Texas State Insurance Department decided that we should turn over to the state, all of the reserves that we had accumulated to pay for potential claims. We had never missed the payment of any claim, and that remains true to this day. We also knew that the state had no department or procedure to process claims so we felt that the people who had put their trust in us would potentially lose their coverage if the state were to take control of the reserves.

In a three-day period, we relocated all reserves to other states, we packed up our business and family possessions, and we moved personnel and everything else to Atlanta, Georgia. There was a huge outcry from the State of Texas but they never pursued us.

Once safely in Georgia, Coy sought to register our company with a regular insurance company, so that we could avoid any further challenges. He built that relationship with Royal Insurance Company. This ended any potential challenges and we continued to pay all claims and to have control of our own business and the reserves.

We returned to Texas in 1990 where I built several more houses and we built our own dream home, a 14,000-square foot house on four acres of property with a pool and tennis court. We were living high. Unfortunately, zoning regulations did not prevent a lot of large retail businesses from building nearby and we decided it was once again time to move on. Coy suggested that we move to Florida, and if so, that he would retire, live off the income from the warrantee business, and let me continue to build houses in Florida.

We moved into a small home in Naples, Florida, while I built a larger home for us in a high-end community. It was necessary at that time for me to work through a locally registered builder as I was not licensed in Florida. Not long after moving into the larger home that I had built, a realtor called me to say that she had someone interested in purchasing our house. We received an offer that we could not refuse on that house. We sold it and we made a huge profit on that single sale. The opportunity before us was undeniable. I quickly bought several more lots and proceeded to make plans to build several more homes.

In 2001, Coy needed to have surgery for a hiatal hernia. Tragically, he did not survive the operation. Stunned and deflated, I moved back to Texas to finish up some business that I had there but I continued to build houses in Naples. I worked through the builder with whom I had previously been associated. That required me to make frequent trips between Florida and Texas to oversee the progress on my housing projects.

I continued to buy and sell houses with a good degree of success. I moved back into one of my houses in Naples. In 2003, through good friends, I met Lee Rattigan. Lee was a CPA with a distinguished career at DuPont. After retiring from DuPont Lee took a position as CFO for Rollins Environmental Company. We were a good match. We married in 2007.

I sold the warrantee business in 2004 which took care of the claims portion; however, my sister still works for me and takes any cancellation or transfer calls whenever they come up. Coy had sold car policies that were never-ending until the mileage ran out. Some people put very little mileage on their cars so I still get a few claims a year. I pay them all!

Looking back, our family was always close and we lived a good life. However, I was always worried about money. We got by, but money was always a concern in my childhood. That influenced me for the rest of my life. The work that I had as a child was hard and on the lower end of the social scale. I could see across the divide, but it was a real stretch. I wanted wealth, security, and a life of class. I was willing to work for it. And I did!

I benefitted greatly from four role models. My mother was a tireless worker, milked the cows twice daily, raised the children, managed the house, and worked as a waitress. She taught me to be willing to work hard and for long hours.

Peggy Hanson, the banker's wife who hired me to baby sit, showed me generosity and the very tempting benefits of a life of wealth. I was hooked!

Jody Ferrer, the owner of Executive Suites, gave me shelter and a job when I had nothing and was alone. She taught me about caring for people and she provided a hand up to get me started.

My Aunt Erma was simply a touch of class. She had a good career, she dressed well, and she socialized in the best circles. She set a standard that I wanted to achieve.

These four role models changed and guided my life. I will be forever grateful to all of them.

For those of you starting out, evaluate the people with whom you come in contact. Consider their actions, their integrity, their generosity, their beliefs, and decide whether or not they represent what you want to be. Knowing what you want to achieve is half the battle. The other half is getting there. You must have the drive, the strength, and the willingness to take a risk if you are going to achieve your dreams.

As a young woman in a "man's world", it was difficult to be taken seriously. When seeking bank loans to finance my construction I found that bankers were unwilling to talk to me without my husband, Coy, being in the meeting. In fact, one banker refused to even look at me during the discussion. Finally, Coy said it is her business, not mine, you make the deal with her.

Getting sub-contractors to work for me was also a challenge. It took time to gain their confidence. Once they learned that I was going to pay them, that I gave clear direction, and that I knew what I wanted, they became loyal supporters. The quality of any construction is dependent on the quality of the sub-contractors that you employ. Always hire the best, treat them with respect, be fair, and pay them well.

Today, fortunately, the workplace environment is different. Women have risen to leadership positions throughout industry and government. There should be no reason why any young woman cannot set high goals, start businesses, become a leader, and be successful.

The success that I have enjoyed has come from several things. I had the personal self-discipline to get the job done. I worked hard, was honest, and I respected my employees. If you are going to succeed you need those qualities.

CHAPTER FOUR

"Don't wait for your ship to come in, swim out to it."
Author unknown

SAILING TO SUCCESS
HENRY HOLZKAMPER

I have often wondered if entrepreneurs are born or if they are taught to be independent? Or perhaps it is simply circumstantial, with opportunity presenting itself to an individual that is willing to chase a dream. Whatever the origin, entrepreneurs must be willing to take risks, must have insight into potential opportunities, must have the ability to react to dire circumstances, and the self-confidence to rebound from failure.

Children grow up having many experiences that seem insignificant or unimportant at the time, but what is learned by those occurrences often becomes useful and helpful in adult life. As a child, my father, a painter, put me to work at the age of thirteen helping him paint. Also, I attended a technical high school where courses in wood shop, electrical shop, welding, and air conditioning all became important to me when I eventually settled into being a landlord with hundreds of apartments.

My first venture into entrepreneurship was at age nine. My buddy Jerry, a year older than me, and I found a wooden wagon and a seat and desk combination in an alley. We put them together, added a square for shade protection, got some paint from my father and built a Kool-Aid stand. Down the block was the turn-around point for the streetcar. We wheeled the stand down there each day with a gallon of Kool-Aid, which actually contained the juice and pulp of a single orange for merchandising effect. We sold it all and grossed $1.25 each day as that was the capacity of our container. To enhance sales, we noticed that the drinking fountain at the turn-around had a valve at the bottom. If we turned it all the way off, people would just turn it back on. But, if we turned it halfway off, making it hard for people to get a drink, people assumed it was low pressure and bought our Kool-Aid. Jerry and I split the money and my father made me put mine in the bank.

Born in 1939 to German immigrants, we lived about a mile north of Wrigley Field in Chicago. My father was a painter by profession, but in the spring of 1929 he bought a frame two flat, which turned out to be worth about nothing because of the depression. He paid the mortgage by shoveling coal or doing just about any other job that would bring in a dollar or two.

When I was born, in 1939 the folks moved up to a brick two flat, renting out the upper floor. In those days, these living arrangements were very common in Chicago and perhaps still are today. This was a blue-collar area and I guess that we were probably lower middle class.

At age 12, my father got me a job stocking shelves in Allen's Paint Store. I lugged the inventory from the basement to the retail level and stocked the shelves. Good exercise but for only $5 per week which my father made me put in the bank. From age 13 to 20 dad made me paint for him. It was not optional. I was paid, but it went right into the bank with me getting a small allowance.

My sister and I grew up under the strict supervision of a characteristic German father and mother. He rigidly believed in living by the Ten Commandments, paying cash for everything, and complete and unwavering honesty.

School was a bit of a struggle for me. I had to work hard at it. Instead of going to the local coeducational high school, my father sent me to Lane Tech, which was a vocational school of

5,000 boys, no girls. Upon graduation, I thought that I had a penchant for engineering and enrolled at the University of Illinois. I soon learned that my interests were misguided when I was invited to leave the University. From there I tried Ripon College in Wisconsin. I was doing okay there but made the mistake of registering for calculus and physics in the same semester. The results were disastrous and I found myself out on the street again. From there I went to Elmhurst College in Illinois and earned a business degree. If at first you don't succeed…

In those days, when you were out of college you were subject to the military draft. As always, I wanted to control my own destiny, so instead of waiting for the draft, I joined the Naval Air Reserve, which committed me to six months of active duty and six years of reserve duty. I had visions of becoming a pilot but here again, I was not qualified for that. I chose aviation electronics. With that training, I flew aboard a P2V which was a plane with two turbojets and two regular jets, looking for enemy submarines. We never found any but we did our duty. Here again, the electronics training eventually became helpful in my yet undetermined future career.

In 1964, I took my first real business job as a sales correspondent for Stewart Warner, a company that sold gauges and instruments. It was fun but restraining being at a desk all day. I quit in May to go to summer school to learn to become a high school teacher. Come September, I did student teaching, and in January 1965 I was employed at North Chicago High School in North Chicago, Illinois. I was a business co-operative Education instructor. I taught students business and how to get employed in the real world, which was a school credit course.

I met Beverly, a school librarian, and we were married in June of 1965, and moved into Chicago in 1966. I too was a teacher at the time, but teaching co-operative education in a Chicago High School at a different school.

Here is where my life began to change. A friend of mine, Darwin Anderson, had recently invested in an apartment building and was making a profit. Characteristically, Darwin was averse to doing anything that involved a lot of work. He told me he had read a book "How to Get Rich in Real Estate" by Robert W. Kent and he suggested that I read it, which I did. That was the start of a new and very successful life. If Darwin could do it, surely, I could too.

In 1966, I bought a four flat. We rented out three of the flats and basically lived rent free in the fourth flat. With Beverly working as a librarian and me as a teacher, and living rent free, we were able to bank one of our salaries every month. The only trick was that I needed to become the janitor for the apartments in my off hours from school. Here is where my training as a painter, and my vocational trades courses came into play. I fixed up the apartments and maintained them by myself.

By 1967 we had accumulated sufficient funds that allowed us to spend the summer high school vacation touring Europe. While there we bought a Porsche 912. Upon return to the States, we still had sufficient funds for me to start investing in more rental properties. At first, I did this with my own money.

Rapidly, I began investing in at least two additional properties each year using OPM. That is a term all entrepreneurs should know. It stands for "Other People's Money". In 1969, I bought six properties with thirty tenants, all on OPM. Sadly, in November of that year Beverly and I divorced.

I rebounded quickly and I married Beth in March of 1970, who also was a teacher, coincidentally, in the same school in which Beverly was a librarian.

Beth and I had two daughters, Heidi, born in 1973 and Holly, born in 1977. We lived in a beautiful house which we had bought in 1974.

Between 1970 and 1979 I bought 27 properties with 405 tenants. I became a full-time landlord and "janitor". I prided myself in doing the work that was necessary, fixing up broken down buildings and renting them for a fair price, and later selling them for a substantial profit. My rapid expansion had been financed by the banks, all of which found me to be a very reliable customer.

Unfortunately, in 1979 I was again divorced. I guess I should have picked a different school from which to harvest my wives. Beth got the house but I, fortunately, retained the rental properties. I'm still close to my children and the four children that they have parented, my grandchildren.

My friend, Jerry, had a 23' sailboat on which I had enjoyed weekends. Eventually, I bought my own 32' sailboat, which I moored and sailed on Lake Michigan. With Beth getting the house, I was essentially homeless. I chose to live on the boat. That was a no-brainer. No rent and a good life.

In 1978 Jimmy Carter became President and interest rates went to 15%++. With my marriage failing, and me having moved onto the boat, I neglected the rental business. I hired a manager, but tenants began to leave. I started to lose some of my properties as well as the attached rehab loans.

Depressed and looking for something new, I went to St. Petersburg, Florida to a boat show. I intended to buy a boat that I could live on and sail it back to Chicago where I could dock it year- round in the Chicago River. In December, 1979, I bought a 43' sailboat. However, on a lark, January found me sailing from Florida to the Virgin Islands. I had income coming in from my remaining rental properties, someone to run them, and I needed a fresh look on life. It took me a week to get to the Virgin Islands.

After spending a number of days by myself, one day I was getting ice on the dock and I met a couple from Chicago that seemed to be admiring my boat. I introduced myself and invited Bill and Denise Kornylak to come aboard and look around. I said help me carry the ice back to the boat and I'll give you the tour. Over casual boat conversation, and, on a whim, I made them an offer. I said, I don't know what you are paying at the hotel, but for the same price you can stay on the boat and I'll throw in the food. A short time later they were back with their suitcases. That was my first charter. They paid me $1800 for three days. Not bad when you consider that I was just sitting idly at the dock.

As spring approached, I needed to sail back to Chicago to tend to business. I found some people willing to be my crew and started north on a journey that would take me to Bermuda, 1,000 miles, then on to New York, another 750 miles, then through the Erie Canal to Buffalo, across Lake Erie, Lake Huron, and Lake Michigan to Chicago. This was a four-week trip.

We encountered stormy weather on the first leg of our trip with seas of about thirty feet. The crew wasn't very happy. One couple was a part of my crew. The husband became ill about 500 miles from Bermuda and equidistant to return to the Virgin Islands. It appeared to be appendicitis with insufficient time to get him to any medical facility. I activated my emergency beacon and about 1:00 AM a plane came overhead to find out what the problem was. They patched me through to a doctor in New York who said the patient had to be removed from the boat to get emergency treatment. They parachuted two medics to the ocean for me to pick up and told me to maintain the same heading and to reactivate my beacon at 11:00 in the morning.

In the morning, another plane arrived from New York and guided us to an oil tanker that had diverted its course, just to pick up the patient. Transfer of the patient to the ship was a real challenge with my new boat banging up against the side of this enormous freighter. We did it. Unfortunately, they would not take his wife too and she had to continue on with us.

We arrived at Bermuda where the patient happily met us for lunch. It was diverticulitis rather than an appendicitis and he had fully recovered. At that point, all of my crew members deserted me. They said they had had enough. I tried to find another crew for the balance of the trip, but to no avail. My only option then, was to make the rest of the trip alone. Having sailed a lot, I knew that even though I slept, I would be sensitive to changes in the wind or other problems and would awaken if need be. I made it to New York where I spent a few days with friends, one of which decided to accompany me for most of the rest of my trip.

I docked in Chicago on June 1, 1980 renting a slip from the Chicago Park District and docking in Burnham Harbor. On a blind date, on June 6, I met Jan Moore, who was employed as a salesperson for promotional incentives. We were a good match. Jan became a 50/50 partner in my rental businesses. In October, the two of us set sail for the Virgin Islands. Spending the winter on a boat in the Chicago Harbor was certainly not an option. We sailed down the Chicago River (having to remove the mast to get under the bridges). Down the Illinois River, the Mississippi River to New Orleans, and then across the Gulf of Mexico, to Key West, and then on to the Virgin Islands. A wonderful trip.

We made that trip back and forth three times in the next several years and basically just lazed about. I still had rental income coming in but, the easy life had to end. If I was going to be really successful I needed to get back to work.

From 1982 to 1990 we acquired more rental properties in Chicago with me being the landlord and handyman.

Over time we had developed a strong friendship with Bill and Denise, the couple that I had first met on the dock In the Virgin Islands. Bill was a successful businessman and he had expressed an interest in investing with me in one or more of my projects. We invested together in a HUD foreclosure of 177 units of which 100 were vacant. I paid $1,100,000 with $250,000 down payment for the property, provided by my investment partner, Bill. The HUD representative then asked where is the fix up money? Entrepreneur that I am I said "look, the government doesn't need the $250,000, why don't you let me use it to fix up the property?" Surprise! He agreed and I started my work. Each time I did a project on the improvement he reimbursed me for the materials to all of the $250,000.

This building had once been an old hotel that the government had converted to HUD apartments. I started by painting and carpeting the halls. Because it started as a hotel it had a large lobby. I put a fountain in the lobby. I put in a security system so that residents could look on their television to see who was wanting to enter or could look at the laundry room, the lobby, and each of the three elevators. I even put a large television antenna on the roof and wired the entire building for cable television. Remember, this is before cable television was a big deal. This allowed all units to have good television reception. I even put beige carpeting on the walls of the elevator which I am proud to say that when I sold the building three years later was still clean. The tenants seemed to appreciate the improved living conditions and tended to take better care of the property.

Jan and I moved in the day that we closed title. We were the first white residents. Now there were some not so stellar residents in these apartments, but overall, they were working people and we got along fine. The problem came when I tried to rent the remaining 100 vacant units. I was asking $300 per month rent which was a good deal for the quality of place that we had. I ran advertisements but as soon as people saw no white faces they walked away. I had no luck with the rentals.

Half of something is better than nothing at all. I ran an ad for "One Bedroom apartments at $150 per month. Still no takers.

By good fortune, in 1982, Poland had a significant uprising causing many Polish people to migrate to the Chicago area. Chicago has always had a large Polish population so this was a natural move for people from Poland. These Polish people had no racial bias and happily moved into my apartments. Some of them spoke English and some did not. I hired one couple, the wife spoke English, to become the manager. I offered her $200 incentive for each new rental that she found. Within a year we were filled up at market rent of $300 per month.

Bill wanted to get out of the business so we sold the building making a million dollars profit. It was probably a bad decision to sell it because it was really making money for us.

From 1982 to 1990 I bought and sold additional properties with good success. I was skilled at fixing them up, and knowledgeable in the world of financing my investments through OPM.

I don't want you to get the wrong impression. I was

not a slum lord. My tenants were blue collar working class people. I provided well maintained and clean facilities at a good price. I incentivized the tenants to do painting of their own apartments with me paying for the paint. I reimbursed tenants for making many improvements, provided lawn mowers and rakes for the yards, etc. I wanted my tenants to be happy with their apartments, and they were. All tenants had my personal phone number. I was the first to purchase a pocket cell phone in 1982 for $4,000 and a dollar a minute. This allowed me freedom, and the ability to be instantly responsive.

In 1989 hurricane Hugo went through the Virgin Islands causing massive destruction. I saw two opportunities. First, it was an opportunity to buy damaged properties cheap, to fix them up, and to rent them or sell them at a profit. Second, I wanted to get into the charter yacht business. I did my research and found that a "Motor Yacht" that took out six passengers, for a reasonable price, would be a winner.

I sold my properties in Chicago and Jan and I, together with our friend Bill, bought an 80' Hatteras Yacht with four bedrooms, four baths, and 3,000 square feet of living space. I changed the dining room to a bedroom and added another bath so that we now could take ten passengers. With a crew, we headed for the Virgin Islands again and opened our charter business as "Paradise Yacht Charters". Paradise was the name of the boat.

We did several test charters just to learn the ropes. At first, Jan did the cooking and we hired a maid to do the heads and beds. The maid situation didn't work out very well. Doing heads and beds, the maid had more contact with the guests than we did. Sometimes that communication was not in the best interest of the business. We fired the maid and hired a professional chef to do the cooking, and Jan took care of the heads and beds. The professional chef was a big success as we won numerous awards for our cuisine. Because there are so many charter boats in the Virgin Islands there are also many professional chefs available at a reasonable price.

Over the next five years we did twenty-two charters that brought in $18,000 – $24,000 per week. With the exception of $7,000 in mortgage payments per month we were basically living free on the boat. At the same time, I was able to pursue potential property acquisitions on the island.

We were very fortunate to have some interesting and famous guests aboard our boat. Early in our business John Travolta and Anson Williams chartered our boat. Their fame, and their satisfaction with our service and accommodations spurred on our success. We also were fortunate to have other celebrities on board such as Andy Griffith and his wife as repeat guests.

Back to my real estate business. There was a large hotel on the island that had been virtually destroyed by Hurricane Hugo, and had remained dormant. I had visions of acquiring the hotel, renovating it and turning it into apartment rentals. Unlike Chicago, this involved meetings with government officials and lots of red tape over a period of several years. We were just about to close the deal in 1995, when Hurricane Marilyn rolled through.

Jan and I tried to ride out the storm on the boat. It was so violent that at times we didn't know which direction we were headed, and we were not sure whether or not we were going to survive the storm. By morning we found ourselves, still on the yacht, but in the middle of a parking lot, well away from the boat basin, with about ten feet of water all around us. Fortunately, the boat was considered totaled by the insurance company. We received full compensation and were allowed to keep the remains of the boat for our own disposal. Within days I sold it for $60,000 to a friend who spent several years rehabbing it. Profits yet to come allowed us to buy it back in 2001 and put a crew on board.

Hurricane Marilyn was probably the best thing that could have happened to us. We had led a wonderful life on the yacht, had met interesting people, we had escaped with our lives and our money, and we were forced to redirect our interests back to real estate. We moved north to Florida in 1996. We settled in Bonita Springs to start looking for rental properties.

In March of 1997 I bought 45 units, all seller financing and credit card down payments. In 1998, I bought 11 units on a credit card and later bought 118 units in a $4 million deal with two friends. I owned 40% and the partners owned 60%. The partners were guaranteed 16% annual return on their investment. That was paid for four years until I bought them out. Today, that property is worth $12 million with a $3.8 million mortgage.

I continued to acquire additional properties, some on my own, and some with partners. There were 115 units in 1999, 2 units in 2000, and 39 units in 2001. Life was great. We bought a fine home in a high end gated community with a full golf and country club membership.

Jan had been my "pal-a-spouse", and business partner for 28 years. In 2007, we decided to make our relationship official and got married with a big reception at the Country Club to which we belonged. That was the best part of 2007.

[Author's Note: Henry, being as assertive as he is, and having practiced the recitals at least two previous times, tried to take charge of the ceremony by reciting the nuptials on his own. The young Priest stopped the ceremony and said, "Henry, you may be old enough to be my father, but I am the Father. You will follow my lead." He did and I guess it worked as they have been married for ten years now.]

Later in that year, the proverbial sh*t hit the fan. The housing boom collapsed. With many of our tenants working the trades, their jobs disappeared. So did our tenants! Between February and November, 25% of our tenants turned in their keys to seek jobs elsewhere. In spite of our outstanding credit, most lenders were unwilling to work with us. I made numerous proposals to lower current payments for larger balloon end payments but to no avail. We went from 350 apartments to about 180 units. We also lost our home in the community that we loved.

Between 2010 and 2012 we were able to refinance and to buy out our former partners. We comfortably managed what we then had left until 2016 when I purchased an $8 million property with 160 rental units. This was totally bank financed with a 25-year mortgage which assumes I will live to age 102. It's a good life that we live in!

Today, I have 329 apartments that are all rented with a waiting list. I could easily raise their monthly rent, but I prefer to give a good value to my tenants. I need no advertising as word of mouth promotes my rentals. I give a fair price, responsive service, and I ensure that the common areas are well maintained. I'm proud to say that all tenants have our personal telephone numbers but we rarely get calls. Our managers handle problems before they get to us.

These investments provide a fine annual income and nice appreciation on the value of my properties.

Earlier, I said that there are many things that happen when growing up that seem to be valueless at the time, but become invaluable later in life. Certainly, my father's demands for living by the Ten Commandments made an indelible mark on my character. Honesty prevails, always. Being forced to save money as a child and to work as a painter during my teenage years taught me some skills that became invaluable as I refurbished my rental properties. And my technical school education that familiarized me with so many different skills that I used during repairs and renovations was also important to my success.

I believe that entrepreneurs must be creative. They must see opportunities and must be able to visualize how they might capitalize on them. I, for one, don't like to take direction from others because I always think that I have a better idea. Perhaps I do or perhaps I don't but that is what makes me so independent. I think that independence and self-confidence are necessary if someone aspires to be an entrepreneur. One must like being in control and willing to take the heat when things go wrong. Even more important, one must be inspired to rebound from failure, to turn lemons into lemonade, to step over hurdles without looking back.

As I reflect on my life, every one of my endeavors has brought me happiness. My achievements have given me great satisfaction. I like to think that I got where I am because I helped people.

As young people strive to become entrepreneurs I encourage them to be proud of what you do, be legitimate, and be fair to your customers. Don't be greedy!

CHAPTER FIVE

"THE BEST WAY TO GET ON IN THE WORLD IS TO MAKE PEOPLE BELIEVE IT IS TO THEIR ADVANTAGE TO HELP YOU"
JEAN DE LA BRUYERE

CIRCUMSTANTIAL LEARNING
YVONNE TUTTLE

My father served in the military during World War II. Being diabetic, he was not eligible for combat functions, so they taught him to be a baker. How strange life is that a physical malady can redirect one's life to a career.

When dad got out of the Army he opened a bakery in Thomasville, Georgia. That became a successful business that essentially involved the entire family.

I was born in Alabama but the family relocated to Thomasville while I was very young. I had a sister, Rebecca, and a brother, John. All of us, including my mother, worked in the bakery. By the age of six, I was able to run the cash register and make change as well as any adult. I even was able to help my father with his taxes.

My dad, John Anthony Miller, was strong willed and self-confident in running the bakery and in life in general.

Even in those days, when girls were not seen as having leadership capabilities, he often told me "Yvonne, you can be whatever you want to be, it just takes hard work and direction, just work for it." I recall him saying "throughout life you will always be climbing a wall unless you are sitting on top. Never accept failure." His guidance motivated me to strive for the top, to be decisive, and to face adversity with courage.

For the last eight years of my father's life he was quite ill. Mom and I pretty much ran the bakery. I think those years of taking charge, having responsibilities, and making decisions established the basis for my competitive drive that led me to success.

When I was seventeen, we closed the bakery. I was a senior in high school and really wanted to go to college, but the money simply was not there. So, in those days, what did a young girl do that can't go to college and needs to find her way in the world? At eighteen, 1965, I got married. And at twenty- one, had a daughter, Katherine. It seemed good at the time.

Now, as a young woman with a child, a house, and no income I had to choose a direction and implement a plan, posthaste. More important, and life changing, I had met eighty-year-old Henry Herbener in 1969. He was an inventor, a first-class entrepreneur, and a person that would become my mentor. Working part-time for Henry, I was able to enroll in classes at Birdwood Baptist College, a two-year school.

Henry had many patents, even two for rotary engines, at a time when rotary engines were just beginning to be thought about. Probably Henry's most profitable invention was girdle stays, which were licensed to Warner Brothers, the largest lady's undergarment company in the United States. Henry's wife, Gabrielle, had complained that her girdle bunched up too much making it uncomfortable. Thus, he invented stays that kept the girdles straight.

Henry taught me so much. He involved me in investing for him, I wrote his patent applications, I helped with his bookkeeping, basically, I was exposed to all aspects of business. Not having finished college, this was the education that I needed.

Henry was averse to flying. At one point, Henry had an opportunity to make a presentation to Saks Fifth Avenue for an innovative new undergarment. Not willing to fly, Henry sent me to make the presentation in New York City. I was petrified. Here was a small-town girl going to New York City to meet with executives of Saks. Henry gave me specific instructions, wear a dark professional suit, heals, and carry a brief case and have a Wall Street Journal folded under your arm. Look professional! It was a successful trip but even more important, it convinced me that, just as my father had said, I could do anything.

I worked for Henry from 1969 until he passed away in 1977, and I will forever be grateful for the education and opportunity that he afforded me. As executor to his estate, I cared for his wife's investments and business affairs until she passed in 1982. His entire estate went to charity.

I married again in 1972 to Tom. This too was not a good choice as the marriage only lasted nine years. Tom was transferred frequently in his job. We moved to Jacksonville, then to Virginia Beach, and then back to Jacksonville. It was not much of an opportunity for me to develop any career of my own.

In 1978, I went to work for a small investment firm in Jacksonville, Florida. As operations manager, I handled all aspects of investment reporting and trading for pension and profit plans, insurance companies, and Union Funds. I worked with many of our clients on portfolio performance. Unfortunately, Tom moved us to Virginia Beach, ending that job for me.

In Virginia Beach, in 1979, I took a temporary receptionist job at an x-ray company as a favor to my neighbor who was the office manager. On the first day, the boss asked me "what are you doing here"? I told him that I was hired as a temporary receptionist until his regular employee could return. He called me into his office to tell me that he had a friend who owns a Trane Air Conditioning Distributorship that needed my skills and expertise. He introduced me and I was hired.

This company was struggling with a poorly planned retirement program that was draining the profits from the company. Because of my background with Henry, and my investment experience, I was hired as controller and business manager. The owner traveled a lot, so we reached an agreement that I would make the decisions and if he disagreed, we would privately discuss them and reach a resolution. I restructured his finances and retirement plans, learned everything that I could about air conditioning and contractors, and I turned the company around in one year.

Just when I was making great progress husband #2 moved us back to Jacksonville. However, Trane corporate had taken notice of the progress that I had made at Virginia

Beach and asked me to go to Houston, Texas as a consultant to open their first hostile buyout/changeover. I opened a 55,000-square-foot facility in 45 days. I hired all of the personnel, set up the accounting systems, leased all of the office equipment, and leased all of the service trucks. We were open for business in 45 days.

I continued to do consulting for Trane traveling to many of the independent and corporate owned distributors all over the country. I had the opportunity to learn the intricate ins and outs of the air conditioning business, service, installation, inventory, job cost, and all aspects of accounting. In 1981, my second marriage ended in divorce.

In 1982, the travel became an issue with my family, so I left Trane and applied for a job as credit manager of Carrier Air Conditioning. As they stated, because I was a woman they would not make me credit manager, but they did offer me the job of director of administration and finance for a small computer division that was providing accounting services to their dealer base. Now I knew nothing about technology, but I did know how to run a business, and how to make money. Their statement was "let the eighteen programmers worry about the technology, you run the business and make a profit". I did.

At one point, the sales manager at the distributor talked me into taking a sales position with lots of incentive guarantees. In my first year, actually, less than a year, I achieved 123% of my quota. No one else made their quota. To my surprise, I was given no bonus because they claimed I had been in the job for less than a full year. I promptly resigned in 1984.

My good friend, Chuck Tuttle, who had also been one

of the salesmen at the Carrier Distributor decided to resign as well in 1984. We decided to go into business together. I had met a contractor who claimed to have a working program for contractors, but in reality, it was not nearly what the contractors needed. Chuck and I entered into an agreement with this company to direct their programming, build, and sell vertical market software to the heating and air conditioning market. The agreement was kept for five years, and the company's reputation was impeccable. The company became very profitable because Chuck and I stayed on top of what had been a poorly run company.

In 1985, I married Chuck, my best friend, my partner, and the father of four children who became my family as well. This enabled us to manage the business and raise our five children, all of whom have now completed college and gone on to successful families and careers. Chuck is the analytical's analytic, and I am the one who makes it happen, which made us a perfect team. I was not afraid to make decisions and to take chances. I had been there before. You just hope that you have made the right decision and that you can get your employees to buy into the plans. Thus, we named our companies "Team Management" in 1990.

After five years we had a buy option which the owner did not honor. He wanted $15 million for a company that we had built with a prior agreement that would have been a fair buyout. Again, we were met with adversity.

At this time, 1990, we decided it was time to open our own company. The former company sued us claiming a non-compete clause, which did not exist. Our agreement stated that if Chuck and I left the company for any reason, we would be compensated 2.5% for three years. But, if we went into competition we would forfeit any ongoing benefits. We fought the lawsuit for the first year of our new business and still made a profit after paying over $100,000 in legal fees. The contract law was later changed in the state of Florida to state that our forfeiture was not the exclusive remedy. Therefore, no matter what the intention is in the contract, if there is a remedy, it must state that it is the exclusive remedy.

We spent six months planning our strategy and purchased the source code that we needed from a New York developer who had no idea how to market and support his product. This allowed us to get to the market, fast track. During that six-month period, I did consulting for contractors all over the country. This was actually the birth of "Team Management Systems, Inc." (a software development entity). Our software included fully integrated accounting, job cost, service dispatching, service management and inventory control. Today, we maintain all these features, as well as remote, two-way communications on multiple operating environments.

To get our company off the ground quickly, I contacted everyone that I knew in the industry, wrote articles for industry publications, and gave educational seminars throughout the country. I attended every distributor dealer meeting to which I was invited. At this time, it was a novelty for a woman to be so involved in the heating and air-conditioning market, presenting fresh new ideas and sound business advice. This created an environment of trust and credibility in the industry. I was the first woman to serve on the Board of the National Association of HVAC Contractors.

Since 1990, "Team Management Companies" have

served contractors all over the United States, the South Pacific, and Australia. We have contracts with major service providers like Service Masters, American Residential Services, American Mechanical Services, and other franchisees.

At one time, we had sixty employees, including programmers, installers, sales people, and office personnel. Y2k was our largest sales year.

Having been in a UNIX environment, which was the universal commercial operating system, we had to change strategies to keep up with the ever-changing technology. The Windows and MAC operating systems began to take over the business environment. Therefore, we were forced to change with the times.

In 2002, we were able to downsize employees and increase profits with the use of the internet. We could demonstrate, sell, and support our software from our desks verses constantly traveling. Chuck partially retired in 2003 and I partially retired in 2012. We both maintain an active interest in the company, but our son Nathan Tuttle now runs the company and is developing software with Cloud applications. Currently, we maintain an in-house staff of twenty employees and utilize a full-time software developer on a contract basis. Recently we have contracted with a large software development group to bring our cloud product to the market.

When I look back on my life, and my success, I think of many influencing factors. First, my father told me that I could do anything that I wanted to do, and I always believed him. If you don't believe in your own ability, you are not likely to succeed, therefore, you should not strive to be an entrepreneur.

I was, out of family necessity, forced to work in the family business at a very young age. Perhaps I could have had more fun playing with the other children, but the lessons and self-confidence that I learned through working in the family business, became invaluable. One must look at the positive side of opportunity rather than the missed entertainment.

I had the good fortune to meet a dedicated mentor who was willing to put trust in me and to teach me as much as he could. One must learn who to trust and when to put faith in their judgement. You must be willing to listen to others and to accept ideas that are potentially better than your own.

Honesty and integrity always come first. Had I not built a strong and favorable reputation throughout the air-conditioning industry our business would not likely have gotten off the ground. At the very least, it would not have grown to the success that we ultimately achieved. Never underestimate the value of honesty and integrity.

Good entrepreneurs know when to cut the cord. I ended two marriages and found a much better life. I quit jobs when they did not suit me. One must be willing to change horses in the middle of the stream. Sometimes one must take risks to correct prior bad decisions. Part of being a good leader is to be able to make lemonade out of lemons.

Agreed, luck is a factor. But, more often than not, you create your own luck. Sometimes luck is hard to recognize until after the fact. It is always part of your life. Capitalize on it! I enjoyed lots of good luck as I worked my way through life.

I have a few suggestions for budding entrepreneurs.

You must be driven, have tenacity, a belief that you can do anything, you must be a doer!

Get it done or get out of the way!

Be a leader and have confidence in yourself. Failure is not an option!

Know what you want in life! Make a plan! Be committed to the plan! Work hard and smart to achieve that plan!

Look professional! Dress as a professional! Submit work as a professional! Act as a professional!

CHAPTER SIX

"IN BUSINESS, TODAY WILL END
AT FIVE O'CLOCK. THOSE BENT ON
SUCCESS HOWEVER, MAKE TODAY
LAST FROM YESTERDAY RIGHT
THROUGH TO TOMORROW."
Lawrence H. Martin

YOU MAKE YOUR OWN LUCK

LEVITAN REALTY
ANN LEVITAN

Ann Couch, (Ann Levitan), was born in Abilene, Texas, in 1942. "My family then moved from Abilene to Lubbock, Texas, when I was three years old. After graduating from high school, I went to college, in Dallas, at Southern Methodist University, starting in a basic Arts &Sciences curriculum. While in college, my family moved to New Mexico, and I only returned to Lubbock for my fiftieth high school reunion."

After graduating from college, I stayed in Dallas to work as secretary to the sales manager at the Holiday Inn. Then after a year or two I moved to Austin, Texas to work for one of the state congressmen. As a family, we were probably upper-middle class. We conserved our money, but we bought what we needed for a good life. We enjoyed country clubs and comfortable living. I had to work for my spending money which left me with a strong work ethic.

My mother had five children, me being the eldest. I had a brother Steve, fifteen months younger than me, a sister that was still-born, another brother James, who survived only three weeks, and a younger sister, Beth. Steve died of heart problems at age thirty-one, leaving me with just one sister. Beth lives in Austin Texas and has been challenged by Multiple Sclerosis since her early forties.

Dad had two years of college, but he quit to earn money to purchase an engagement ring for my mother. My father was rather quiet. Mom played the major role in my life as she was a more aggressive personality. She was the guiding factor for me. Mom had a teaching certificate but like most families of that era my father did not want her to work. It was a matter of personal pride to be the sole provider at that time. In those days, people often looked down on families in which the wife worked.

Dad was more of an entrepreneur than anything else. He bought, and built, and sold numerous businesses. His last business was one that made explosives for mining and other uses. He eventually sold that business with a contract to stay on for five years as a consultant. This afforded memberships in country clubs and my own Debut, which was a big deal in those days.

As far as my mother's influence, I recall when I was in the third grade, I said to Mom, "Look at how lucky I am by winning all of these awards and trophies." She said, "luck doesn't just happen, you make your own luck in life." I never forgot that statement, and I think it was a defining moment in my life when I realized that you get out of life what you put into it. From that point on, I set goals for what I wanted to achieve, and I went after those goals.

I recall in the seventh grade seeing someone win the Daughters of the American Revolution Award (DAR). I wanted that award! That person was editor of the school newspaper paper and I felt that surely, being an editor, was an avenue to achieve my goal. I worked for the school paper and eventually became the Editor. I also ran for student body president, being the first female to seek that position. It was a close race, but I lost. Oh yes, I did get the DAR Award.

In high school, I was not interested at all in the home economics courses which focused on sewing and cooking classes. I concentrated on typing and shorthand classes even though, at that time we still had to handwrite all our schoolwork. In the 1950's, most of us did not have a typewriter in our homes. My grandmother had an old key driven typewriter on which I practiced. I could really type fast and won the high school Texas State Championship. These lessons proved invaluable in my adult life, opening the door to many career opportunities.

Following high school graduation, I went to college at Southern Methodist University where I achieved a Bachelor of Business Administration degree. I decided to focus on business administration as that degree also included a teaching certificate.

While in high school, I worked in a women's clothing boutique. Merchandising was not my forte, so I was confined to the backroom work. I did, however, get to assist at the markets, which gave me great insight into the business. Most important, I learned the skills of treating customers with respect and care.

In 1964, as a student teacher of high school typing, shorthand, and business math, I found myself in a difficult situation. School integration laws had just passed and the school that I was working in was dramatically changed. Integration was the right direction but the students coming into the school had insufficient prior schooling in the subjects for which I was trained to teach. I therefore found myself having to teach at a lower perceived grade level, rather than the high school level for which I had been trained. Coupled with the realization that I could make more money doing the work rather than teaching it, as well as the fact that I didn't enjoy the challenge, I decided not to pursue a teaching career.

At one point I took a job in Dallas working for the largest Holiday Inn. I coordinated the meetings, bookings, room assignments etc. This happened to be the facility that housed the visiting and the local professional sports teams. I got to know many of the players. When the Cowboys were playing they would stay at the hotel for the weekend. I had to know who the big guys were that couldn't stay in a small bed, who could not room with each other, who were the rounders that would stay out beyond curfew, etc. The rounders had to have rooms far away from the coach so that he didn't catch them. It was an interesting and exciting job.

With my bachelor's degree in hand, I went to Austin, Texas to work as secretary to one of the congressmen. After a year I left that job and worked as secretary to the treasurer of an investment firm. My typing and shorthand got me the job, but I was also very strong in math.

A friend of mine, in Dallas, decided to open his own stock brokerage firm. He recruited me to be Secretary to the President of the firm and gave me an offer that I could not refuse. He taught me a lot about trading stocks. I handled transactions and the regular letters to investors updating their portfolios etc. I remember watching the ticker tape with him one day and he said, "You may know what all of the PE ratios, etc. are for all of the stock names going across that board, but just remember, that it is still a crap game!"

It became worrisome to the owner that I was taking trade orders without a license. He was frequently out of town, so I had to take the orders. He asked me to take a correspondence course from the New York Institute of Finance. The deal was, I would pay $100 up front to take the course. If I passed, he would reimburse me. Now think about that, the men my age were sent to New York for the six-week course, all expenses paid. I had to work my job, go home at night to study and complete the assignments, not to mention taking care of his kids and pets when he was gone. That is the way work went for young women entering the workforce in the early 1960s. I passed and got my broker's license. I worked there three years.

While working at the stock brokerage firm, I met and fell in love with George, a labor attorney. He had previously worked for Jimmy Hoffa, but by the time I met him he had "switched sides" and was representing management, not the union. He represented many large companies including Playboy, Southland Corporation (7-11 stores), trucking companies, etc. He lived primarily in Chicago, belonged to numerous clubs and was well known in the better restaurants. For a period of months, he would send me first class tickets to fly to Chicago on the weekends. Eventually, I moved to Chicago, where we had separate apartments. George and I were engaged but never married.

I then took a position with an investment counseling firm in Chicago, as Assistant to the Chairman of the Board. That company managed three large mutual funds, various pension funds, etc. Eventually the firm acquired Chicago Title & Trust, and my boss now was Chairman of the Board of everything. It was a typical corporate setup where, even I, had my own secretary!

George had a vacation home that he had built in Acapulco, Mexico. We went there often on holidays. On one trip, while relaxing at a hotel pool bar with friends from Chicago, we met a nice guy who had just started working in Chicago. It happened to be Steve Levitan, (Steve and his wife were attempting to restore a weakening marriage. Ultimately that didn't work.)

George liked Steve and invited him and his wife to come to his home for dinner. He sent the car and driver to transport them to his home and back. It was a lovely evening and then George invited them both to come to a big birthday party for me at one of the top disco night clubs in Acapulco. Steve came alone for a short period of time, as his wife did not want to come. Once we were back in Chicago, Steve wanted to reciprocate and invited George and me to be his guests for dinner at one of the better restaurants which he frequented.

A day or two after that dinner, I stopped by George's apartment to retrieve something. I found George on his bed holding the phone to his ear. I picked up the phone and asked who was on the line. It was one of George's friends and business partner. He told me that he had been talking to George, and suddenly there was just silence. I then said, "Well, I am standing right beside him, and he is dead," George had been out jogging that afternoon and died of a massive heart attack at the age of forty-two.

A day or two later Steve received a call from the maître de at the restaurant where we had dined. He said to Steve, "You know that guy you brought to dinner the other night? There's a big article in today's paper about him. He died."

Steve, being very concerned for my well-being, often joined me for late night drinks and he tried very hard to find me a potential spouse. He introduced me to numerous fine men. Even though I was earning a good living and enjoying a rather comfortable life; I was now in my early thirties and thinking that it was time for me to find a spouse. I was dating three different men that Steve had introduced me to at that time. While all of them were nice and of comfortable means, not one of them really moved me. I decided to go to Europe for a vacation and sort things out in my mind. While in Europe, Steve called me nearly every day to see what I was thinking. I finally said, "You know Steve, of all of the men, the only one that I miss is you." I returned to Chicago and married Steve in 1975.

Steve was in the clothing business as a sales representative for a Montreal clothing company. I became pregnant with our daughter Peyton and I quit the investment business.

In the early 1980s, Steve, Peyton, and I moved to New Jersey. At that time, Steve was involved as a partner in a men's high-end overcoat manufacturing company in

Montreal. He served as President of the U.S. operations and we opened an office in Manhattan. This was the age of computers and I had become very competent in handling the records, reports, etc. for Steve's business. The clothing factory even started using the programs that I had set up for his reports. I worked with Steve in the Manhattan office until 1992.

At that time, I was fifty years old and thought that a retirement life of fun and games in Florida would be great. We moved to Florida and Steve continued to work for another six years. He commuted to New York and he traveled throughout the country selling clothing.

As it turns out, "I am not miss goody home-maker". "I was bored as Hell." I decided to go back to work. Because of my computer knowledge, and my math skills, and my tax knowledge, I found a job with H&R Block. I only worked three days per week but became "Rookie of the Year".

Now comes the entrepreneur part of my career. In 1994, a friend encouraged me to get my real estate license. As an agent, one works for a real estate broker. However, agents are paid only on commission. Essentially one is in business for him or herself. I became very successful selling out all of the condominium units in their primary building in the first year.

With the success that I was having, Steve suggested that I get my broker's license and open my own brokerage. To become a broker, one must have been an agent for at least a year, plus courses that come in sections taking seventy-two hours of training, pass that test, then another sixty hours of instruction and another test. I passed!

The lady that I worked for offered to have me become a

partner with her in the brokerage that I had been working for. I was reluctant to do that because we had different philosophies as to how the business should be run. She was looking for large scale real estate operations while I was interested in a specialty or boutique type business.

I estimated to Steve that it would take $50,000 for me to start my own business. He said, "go for it". In 1997 I opened the Levitan Company on Route 41 in Naples. Having a background in computers, math, taxes, typing, etc., I had no trouble doing all of the necessary support operations for the business. I sold during the day and after dinner I worked until midnight on the various administrative functions. Within the first year I made back more than the initial investment.

I had an agent, Tiffany McQuaid, working for me since the year 2000. In 2008, I asked her to partner with me and for five years she did so. During that time, we were known as the Levitan-McQuaid Real Estate Company. In 2013, we parted on good terms as she wanted to focus on real estate in the downtown Naples area, while I preferred the upscale housing market in North Naples. My philosophy is that you must select your market and focus on being the best in that particular area. It is too easy to spread yourself too thin, which often results in business failure.

The key to my success was focusing on the in higher end communities. Volume, or income, is directly related to the number of agents that I have working for me. I personally was able to average thirty transactions per year. A transaction is either a listing or a sale. In addition, my agents averaged another thirty or more transactions per year for which I also earned a percentage.

Much of my success is related to referrals. Often referrals come from other realtors who are not working in the area. Also, friends and past clients frequently recommend me to someone. I have always preached in my business "Take the high road". I think that honesty, integrity, and professionalism are the real keys to success. Even if you have to bite your tongue and swallow a bad deal, it is worth it to keep your high reputation. Looking back, I think that my early dress shop experience made me recognize that the key to good service is to make the customer feel special.

At one time I had as many as twenty-five agents working for me. That was too much as ultimately, I am legally responsible for the agent's actions. I needed to be involved in too many of their deals. Today, I have thirteen agents working for me.

Steve retired from his clothing career in 1999 and in 2000 earned his real estate agent license. Daughter Peyton also has her license and has worked for me since 2004. She will eventually take over the business, but I don't see myself walking away in the near future.

The normal real estate transaction has a 6% commission tied to it. Of that, 3% goes to the listing agency and 3% to the selling agency. Commission arrangements for listers and sellers vary by agency and by length of service.

We have been successful for many reasons. First, we stay focused on our market. Second, we have very low overhead because I do the administrative work. Third, we do our own printing for our ads. Fourth, we depend heavily on direct mail and the internet. Fifth, we have a good reputation. Most of our leads come from referrals based on how well we have handled other client's transactions.

This sounds as though life is easy. It is not! Success is largely influenced by the real estate market. When the housing market gets low or interest rates get high, sales may disappear. One must have sufficient assets to weather the market down-turns.

If I were to advise others about the real estate business, I would start by saying that you must have enough funds to live for at last a year. Sales don't usually come fast. People shopping for homes tend to look for the older and more experienced agents. Specifically, the high-end shoppers tend to put their trust in the older, more experienced agents.

I think that some people are born with a desire to achieve. It is just in their nature. I was always achievement oriented. Certainly, environment helps in establishing each person's motivation, but, if you look at siblings, they often go in different motivational directions. If you are not highly motivated to achieve, then entrepreneurialism is not for you.

For young people today, I fear that they have not had the discipline to work the hard and long hours that it takes to be an entrepreneur. Our generation grew up with parents who endured the great depression. They knew the value of the dollar and they knew the importance of hard work and commitment to a job. Their commitment could not help but rub off on us. The successes of our generation have made life appear easier to the young people of today. I don't think that they have the drive that was implanted in us. Life is not easy. Work hard!

CHAPTER SEVEN

"The road to success is filled with women
pushing their husbands along."
Thomas R. Dewar

Roman, Inc.
Ron Jedlinski

There was never a question about a career. Ron was to be an entrepreneur from his very beginning. From the time he was six years old he was already a figurine collector, mostly cowboys and Indians. These came in handy when his father's gift shop was short on inventory and they needed merchandise to sell.

Ron, and his siblings, Arlene, Tony, and Loraine, lived in a typical ethnic community of Polish, Catholics. All of the extended family members generally lived within a few blocks and family drop-ins were the norm. They were middle class or perhaps a little above that. Ron's father, Roman Jedlinski, was an artist. He basically painted and sold his artwork to support the family. When Ron was just a child, his father began silk-screening his work with the help of Ron. Together in the basement they would produce

150 copies of his art at a time and sell them to retail outlets for $18 a dozen. It was a very small profit but not much was needed in those days.

With World War II winding down, Ron's mother, Leona Jedlinski encouraged Roman to open a small gift shop. The shop dealt in painted signs, small giftware, and seconds that they bought from Haeger Pottery for resale. They also sold Christmas cards that they bought 21 in a box for $1. They sold them for a nickel, making the extra nickel on the 21st card. Ron worked in the store as a child but also bought toys and comics from distributers and resold them from his wagon.

Ron's father agreed that Ron could go to college and he would help support him if Ron would continue to help in the store. In addition, Ron received a small scholarship and attended Northwestern University. He later received a full scholarship and completed his bachelor's degree as well as receiving a commission in the United States Navy through NROTC. Throughout college Ron continued to work for his father in the store and by selling merchandise to retail outlets. By the time he graduated he had about 150 customer businesses.

Ron is not an artist, but he has taste and an eye for what might sell. Even in college he would write little verses, have them printed on plaques or plates, and sell them. He was always highly sensitive to trends and a visionary in trinkets, religious items, collectables, and general gift items.

In those days, all men were subject to the draft for military service. Ron chose NROTC in college and with his commission he served his two years as a supply officer. He went to supply school at a fort in Georgia where the rule was that the higher you graduated in your supply course the better your choice of where you would be deployed. Ron graduated 5th out of 250 and chose a stores ship homeported in Barcelona.

When Ron was honorably discharged from the Navy in 1963, he started his own business selling many of the same things that he had while in college. The difference was that he was now in business for himself, paying a small rent to his father for some space to warehouse merchandise, calling on accounts, and taking all of the risk. He was able to renew his relationship with the accounts with whom he had previously dealt. His business was started.

While stationed in Barcelona, Spain Ron arranged for his first importation. I started with religious figurines which were very realistic. They were glass-eyed statues such as the head of Christ with crowns of thorns, crystal tears, eyes that followed you, and lots of blood. When the shipment arrived, my father questioned where will I sell all of this stuff? Unrecognized by me, the market was turning away from that type of religious merchandise. By sheer luck, as others dropped out of these lines of goods, I was able to fill in the gap. It was a start.

There was a saying, "God can't be everywhere, that's why he invented mothers". As an example of Ron's vision and aggressiveness, he rewrote that little saying, "Mothers can't be everywhere – that's why God invented Grandmothers". He had that put on a plaque and ordered 5,000 of them. He paid $1.20 and sold them for $3.00. He sold between 50,000 and 100,000 thousand of them. Obviously, he had a sense of what would sell and was willing to make a commitment.

Wiebolt Stores, a Midwest department store chain,

allowed Ron to inventory a small counter of his miscellaneous goods and write the replacement orders each week. This progressed to other department stores, including Marshall Field. By then he was also displaying at the Chicago Gift Show and making a name for himself in the industry.

He borrowed $100,000 from the bank and opened a 3,000 square foot warehouse, his first of several. Behind his warehouse was a liquor business that discarded their empty boxes in the back. To save money, Ron would retrieve these boxes and pack his merchandise, mostly religious items, in them. When packages would be delivered people would joke, "here comes the holy spirits".

In 1970, he went to the gift show in Italy. There he met Ugo Fontanini who made exquisite nativity scenes and figurines. Fontani's workmanship was beyond any other and the two of them struck up a relationship that continues to this day. Ron developed the idea to name the different figurines and to develop small stories about each, making them collectables. He secured exclusive rights to the line for the western hemisphere, and still has that today. This has been one of the many highlights of the business as Fontani Collector's Clubs developed, some of which continue to this day. It was through Ron's efforts to publish the small bios on each of the figurines and to build interest in these Nativity Scenes that made the sales explode.

The Fontanini business has existed for 150 years, but this was starting a new chapter. Ron recognized it for the best molds and the best detail. This line would be considered one of the main cornerstones of Roman's business, having lasted as their product line since the 1970s to this day. Roman sells the Fontanini line to many outlets and to the Disney Parks each Christmas. Disney loads up at Christmas but always promptly sells out.

Another strong line was Seraphim Angels. These were sculpted by Gaylord Ho, a highly esteemed artist. The key to any of these figurines is the sculptor. Roman carried this line for 15 to 18 years but young people no longer see the value in collectables. They don't buy fine china or commemorative plaques. Basically, what once was called a collectable is now called a dustable. That is the way that business can change, and one must be prepared to react to the market, to take your lumps and to move on to something new. Much of Ron's business grew during a time when collectables were highly popular and sought after. In the 1970s, Lladro, Royal Dalton, and Hummel led the way to the popularity of collectables. The trend at that time toward collectables opened the door to much of his success.

"It is said that all success stories have an element of luck. If good people are an element of luck, I was surrounded by them: good parents, a good wife, good friends and relatives, (some of whom came to work for Roman), and good customers." My younger brother, Tony, thirteen years younger, became a key player in our business. Tony is brilliant. He handled all of the technology that kept our company going. In addition, Tony planned and supervised the construction of our warehouses.

With those people backing him up, Ron could concentrate on the creative development of product lines. He was/is, an idea man. He can visualize an opening in the market, he can see religious trends, he can feel the emotional draw of the figurines that he and his team develop, and he has the courage to take risks with large orders. Ron also has concentrated on high quality products with fine workmanship at affordable prices. Basically, he created the lines, hired professionals to do the design, negotiated the manufacturing, took the risk, and sold the product. That is entrepreneurship!

Not everything is always a success. There is a gospel according to Roman. "If you never make a mistake, you're not trying enough things." Probably our best example of that was a line of snake ashtrays that we produced.

In our early years we were fortunate to do business with, and get to know, Arvid and Katherine Strom. They owned three of the best gift shops in Chicago called Ono's Gift Shops. Ono's Gift Shop carried all of the best lines. People didn't think of figurines as collectables in those days, they were basically nice novelties. Ono's gift shop carried all of the best lines. They had animal figurines imported by the Sadek Company and made by Kowa in Seto that were very popular. Arvid was a successful big game hunter and an amateur herpetologist. He convinced me that the market would buy reproductions of the world's deadliest snakes. These coiled snakes could hold an ashtray as a symbol of the dangers of smoking. It sounded reasonable.

We had an expert from the Museum of Natural History sculpt the Indian Spectacled Cobra and the Eastern Diamondback Rattlesnake. We casted them in oxalite, a bonded marble dust and poly-resin in Italy. Our agent had to find women who didn't believe in the Evil Eye to paint them. We put them on the market and scared the hell out of our customers. They were so realistic that people would walk out of our showrooms. I finally dumped them on a carnival supplier in Colorado. Yes, mistakes happen but one must take their lumps, accept the loss, and move on to something new. Having the capital behind you to be able to take a loss is a key to entrepreneurial survival.

Around the year 2,000 Ron found an opportunity to be a leader in the pre-lighted Christmas tree business. While he had fine products and potentially great volume, there were certainly drawbacks. In comparison to the small items that were stocked for the figurines, these were very bulky items requiring lots of storage space. Also, they were so seasonal, that the business was concentrated in a very short period of time. On top of that, everyone was competing in that business making it highly competitive. Without any copyrights, Ron walked away from the business.

An amusing story is about a Saint Anthony's statue. We all know the story behind the Saint Joseph Statue, that was rumored to help you sell your house if you buried it in the yard upside down. Of course, there was no truth to this rumor, but it caught hold because of some media exposure that started the popularity. The mass media can drive anything, many times without even intending to do so. A simple comment on the news may get the attention of people who are gullible enough or suspicious enough to try anything.

However, some lady sent Ron a Saint Anthony's Statue holding a heart, and she claimed it had helped people find love. Ron jumped on the idea and produced a line that he hoped would get media recognition and catch fire the way that Saint Joseph did. The media didn't jump on it, but still today, some lonely hearts find comfort in having one of these statues. The line just plods along.

Newness is a key factor in the giftware business. We

must always be cycling out declining items and replacing them with new ideas. New colors, new styles, new figurines, new sayings, new everything. Today we carry about 8,000 stock keeping units, of which we transition about 2,000 each year.

To support our inventory, we originally started with a 3,000 square foot warehouse. As we grew, Tony Jedlinski built larger and larger facilities for the business. In 1987 he built a 155,000 square foot warehouse in Roselle, Illinois, and then in about 2,000 a 500,000 square foot warehouse and office complex in Addison, Illinois.

Each line generally has a life cycle of one to five years. New ideas come from trade shows and vendors who are looking for an outlet for some idea that they have. Occasionally, ideas come out of the blue from some interested party. A good example is a line of Story Bracelets. A woman along the Mexican border connected with some people in Mexico who were making beaded bracelets. Each bead was made differently, each telling its own part of the story of the life of Christ. This has been a very popular line and continues to sell thousands of these bracelets each year.

Roman's business consists of about 50% religious items. They specialize in baby gifts, wedding gifts, engagement gifts, anniversary gifts, and a big category is sympathy gifts. Essentially, their gifts take a person from cradle to grave.

At the peak of Roman's business, they generated about $140 million in revenue per year. At one time Roman employed as much as 400 people, but today it employs 80 regular employees plus about 70 representatives. In the early days all of the representatives were representing only Roman. Today they need to represent multiple companies in order to generate sufficient income for themselves. With the decline of collectables and the departure from Christmas trees, and other consolidations, Roman still does about $40 million healthy dollars per year. Ron remains the dominant shareholder and is actively involved in the business on a daily basis, from a semi-retirement location. His son-in-law, Dan Loughman, is the President of the company today and has been for about 15 years.

When asked about the keys to Ron's success, he emphatically said "Do the right thing! Don't lie, cheat or steal! This is the seventh chapter and it is interesting that the key element of success in every case has been honesty. That should tell us something. I would like to think that honesty would be automatic, but it is not in all businesses.

Writing this chapter, I can't help but think about the emotional feelings that must go through an entrepreneur's mind when he or she decides to back off of their daily involvement in the business. It is inevitable that businesses end or that the owner ages out of the active business life. An entrepreneur's business is like a child that was born of this individual. It is the pride and joy of his or her own creative genius. It has been their life and has occupied the vast majority of their waking hours. How does one come to grips with walking away? How much control can be relinquished? How much control should be retained? How to replace the void in one's daily activity? An entrepreneur's business is not like a corporate job where you work for shareholders, give it your all and then someone else takes over. This is personal and all entrepreneurs should be planning for when they will walk away and how they will do it.

CHAPTER EIGHT

**"DESTINY IS NOT A MATTER OF CHANCE,
IT IS A MATTER OF CHOICE"
AUTHOR UNKNOWN**

RADIO STATIONS
ARNOLD LERNER

Success as an entrepreneur is dependent on three things. First, you must have some luck. Second, you must be able to see opportunities that others don't see. And third, you must have the courage and drive to go after these opportunities. Sure, there are many other factors, but those were the overriding influences that led to my own success. But one does not have to be born with these attributes. They can be learned. I didn't have any particular direction as a boy, and even as a young man. I knew nothing about radio stations; but a set of circumstances presented themselves, and with support from my father and good advice from a neighbor, I stumbled into a rewarding career of, along with partners, owning and operating twenty radio stations in twelve markets.

Born in 1930, (before television) I grew up in the

Philadelphia suburb of Drexel Hill, Pennsylvania. In those days, families huddled around the radio at night to listen to mysteries and comedy shows. I was a Jewish boy in a gentile neighborhood and a year younger than my classmates. Yes, there was some antisemitism, but I had the good fortune of being raised by loving parents in a happy home. And although my first decade of life was during the great depression, we never went hungry

My father was born in in 1889 in what is now known as the Ukraine, and he immigrated with his family to the United States when he was six years old. His family settled in a farm community in southern New Jersey. At age thirteen, my father and a buddy left the farm and went to New York City to make their own ways in the world. Eventually he linked up with his brothers and started a woman's coat and suit manufacturing business in Philadelphia. His formal education stopped at sixth grade, but he was intelligent and talented and learned from experiencing the real world. My mother was the daughter of a Rabbi, was fifteen years younger than my father, grew up in Philadelphia during the "roaring 20s", and without any doubt was the boss of our home.

At seventeen years of age, I graduated from the Upper Darby Senior High School. Interestingly, at that time (1947) we were taught that THE basic law of physics was the "conservation of matter", meaning that matter is indestructible Then the United States dropped atomic bombs on Hiroshima and Nagasaki, ending World War II turning some matter into energy. This law now became the "conservation of matter and energy" and it has been a different world ever since. I went to the University of Pennsylvania's Wharton School of Business as an undergraduate. I nearly flunked out my first year but by the time I was a senior, I was on the Dean's List. I graduated in 1951 with a bachelor's degree majoring in marketing, and in 1974 received a master's degree from Boston University's Metropolitan College in what was then called Liberal Studies.

I was a naïve kid with no strong personal goals, so following college, I worked for my father, assuming that I would just grow into and eventually take over his business. Both while growing up, and then spending three years watching my father solving problems in the conduct of his business, I received my advanced business degree. Clearly, my father was the biggest influence in my life, but here is where luck came into play.

First, my father was able to sell his half of the business for a god price to his brother partner. This was a really good thing, both because the marketplace for ladies clothing was changing with less demand for ladies' suits, and because my father's health was deteriorating. Second, we had a close friend, a neighbor, Lou Pollar, who owned a radio station in Chester, Pennsylvania. He became the second most influential person in my business life. He encouraged me to look into the radio station business. This was in the early 1950s at the beginning of television. It was generally assumed at that time that the advent of television would bring the demise of all radio stations. Who would want to listen to the radio when you could also have a picture? Radio stations became very inexpensive to purchase.

A story. When I was working for my farther, the inside

joke in the clothing business was that there are basically five seasons, one of which was the slack season when there was little to do. My father and our next-door neighbor, Lou Pollar conspired to keep me busy in the 1952 slack season, and so I went to work for Lou's radio station for about a month. Thus, my first job in radio was in Chester, Pennsylvania, selling advertising on commission. Also, this is where I made my first sale. What a thrill.

This was in 1952 at a time when most stations still had house bands for music. The station's regular format was to primarily play records that appealed to black listeners, Chester's population being about 40% black. The station was approached by a newly formed country music band of musicians who had just come home from the war in Korea, to be its band. So we had a country music band working at a black programmed radio station. They made a record which reflected both music styles. The band was Bill Haley and The Comets. And the song was "Rock Around the Clock", the first Rock and Roll record, and I believe the source of the word "Rock" in the name of this music style.

By 1954 my father was totally retired. In 1955, I was hired by Macy's Department Store to go through its executive training program, which I did and then became and assistant buyer of men's shirts and pajamas. Macy' Herald Square store was at that time, the largest retail store in the world. With nine selling floors in a building occupying a full New York City block from 34th Street to 35th, and from 7th Avenue to Avenue of the Americas (6th Avenue). I was there for a year learning retail from the experts. This turned out to be extremely helpful for my career in radio, since most of my future advertisers were retailers, and I could talk their language.

In 1956, Lou Pollar arranged for me to work for WCMS, a country music station in Norfolk, Virginia as an advertising time salesman. I think he wanted to find out if I really could sell time. I could. Then Lou put together a group of investors to buy Radio Station KOMA Oklahoma City for $300K. This was a heavily discounted price accepted by owners that believed that TV would kill radio as a mass medium and that radio's best days were over.

W borrowed $200K from a bank and invested about $100,000. My share was about a third, the same as Lou Pollar, which I borrowed from my father. I moved to Oklahoma to attend the closing and to work at the station. I remember clearly my hand sweating profusely as I wrote the check for the $300,000 purchase price. By then, I was pretty good at selling advertising, but I still had a lot to learn about running radio stations. I was lucky enough to hire as General Manager, Raymond Ruff, a long-time sales manager at a competitor station, who had been trained by Westinghouse Broadcasting, one of the best run radio group owners in the country. He was the one who really taught me the business, how to operate stations and how to buy and sell them. Then, luck smiled on us again.

I mentioned earlier that the advent of television was considered the death sentence for radio stations. Todd Storz, who owned a radio station in Omaha, and who tended to spend a fair amount of time in pubs, observed that while in bars, people played the juke boxes constantly, often the same songs over and over again. He realized that there might be a market for music on the radio and he developed the "Top

40" list, which survives to this day, and started playing the top songs on and hourly basis. It worked! Radio stations instantly became more valuable.

After owning KOMA for only two years we accepted an offer for the station that was too good to refuse...from the same Tod Storz. We sold the station for $600,000, twice what we had paid for it. Stations that previously sold at a discount were now selling at a premium. We paid off the bank its $200K loan, and our original $100K investment had magically produced $400,000! My share was about $133K. I repaid the loan from my father and enjoyed having $100K in my bank account. At 28 years old in 1958 this was a lot of money. I thought to myself, "This sure beats the Hell out of ladies clothing".

I decided to stay in the radio station business as a career. Raymond Ruff and I, and another investor, found a station for sale in San Bernardino, California that looked almost too good to be true. It turned out that it was. Generally speaking, one can approximate the radio advertising dollar potential of a market by taking the total retail sales of the market and applying a factor of 5 or 6% of retail sales for total advertising dollars, and then 5 or 6% of total advertising dollars for radio dollar potential. This number gets adjusted, but it is a good stating point. Looking at this market and checking the sales of the other stations in the market it appeared that we had a potential winner. Wrong! We almost got killed.

What we did not fully appreciate was that San Bernardino was a stopping place to get gas on the way to Palm Springs from Los Angeles. The retail sales of this area were significantly skewed by this drive-through traffic and therefore, the advertising potential for the market that we had calculated was not there.

I can't stress enough the importance of doing a thorough due diligence before investing. We were lucky again. In the radio business we often benefit from what we refer to as the Greater Fool Theory. Often when you want to sell a station, along comes a fool even greater than you, to buy you out. Fortunately for us someone meeting this description came along and bought the station from us. We broke even and learned a great lesson.

As in every business, there are agencies that specialize in the sale of radio stations. I began working through one of these agencies and started buying radio stations. I purchased a small station in Newport, Rhode Island which worked out well. For the first time I was the General Manager. By then, my partner from Westinghouse had been recruited away to a very high position covering both radio and newspaper in Oklahoma City. Now I had just one partner left.

Three years later, we bought an AM station in Lowell Massachusetts. This was an estate sale and it required that I also take ownership of the co-owned FM station. Since they brought in no revenue, FM stations were virtually worthless at that time. However, I was able to convert this monaural FM station to a 50,000 watt stereo station which covered Boston. The potential for advertising revenue was terrific. Thirty-three years later I was able to sell that initially worthless station for $20M.

Over the years, I was a partner in twenty stations in twelve markets, small, medium, and large. I didn't always have the same partners in each location. As the business grew, I began to recognize outstanding employees by making them partners in future stations that we purchased. I saw this as a form of insurance, protecting the investments that I had. By sharing the business, I could sleep well at night knowing that my managers were honest and capable. To this day (I just celebrated my 90th birthday), some of them still call me to see how I am getting along. There is a lesson here for any entrepreneur. The best way to protect your investment is to hire well and then incent these people to do the very best job of which they are capable. My father used to say that you can never make as much money by yourself as you can when people are making it for you.

My younger brother came in as a partner when I bought the Lowell station, worked there, and learned the business. Some years later, we applied to the FCC to construct an FM station in Media, Pennsylvania, in competition to two other applicants. We lost in the first round, but we won on an appeal and received the permit and license to build and operate a 50,000 watt stereo station. He was living in Philadelphia at the time and became the new station's General Manager. Once again, we turned a suburban FM station into a high-powered station that could cover a major market, tis time it was Philadelphia.

When I look back, I had the benefit of three great mentors: My father who did not tell me how to live my life, rather he showed me, and backed me financially. Lou Pollar who took an interest in me and encouraged me into radio. And Raymond Ruff, who taught me the radio business and made me a professional. I did not start out with any particular goals in mind, but I listened to my mentors, learned from my experiences, recognized opportunities, and was willing to take risks to pursue the opportunities that seemed to pop up. I recognized opportunities, and I was willing to pursue the opportunities that seemed to pop up.

How can I advise young entrepreneurs today? Today, you must know more. You need a wide, focus. In the old days you could be a generalist or a specialist. Today, you must be both and you must be good at both. You should try to know what is going n in the world in seemingly unrelated disciplines and look for connections that others have not seen or properly exploited. And at the same time, try to become very good at something. Pursue your interests. Go with your strengths. Fulfill your potential.

To succeed, it helps to be a good judge of character. I can't emphasize enough the importance of character, yours, and that of your associates. Finding good people and keeping them effective and happy is crucial. Treat them honorably and, if they are the right people, they will reciprocate.

In the radio broadcasting business, we deliver audiences to advertisers. We attract these audiences by providing news and entertainment that people want to tune in for. If we honestly fulfill our part of this contract, audiences will love us, they will remain with us and we will be profitable. And we will have a happy life.

CHAPTER NINE

"SUCCESS IS A JOURNEY, NOT A DESTINATION"
BEN SWEETLAND

THE COMMON LINKS

The purpose of this book is to find common links among very successful entrepreneurs that may have made the difference between failure, moderate success, or even exceptional success. Hopefully, the reader will have gleaned some gems of wisdom that may have a positive influence on his or her own career.

Obviously, hard work is a given for success in anything. There were, however, more important issues that must be discussed.

Honesty

Every subject dwelled on honesty. Bud Dahbura, "Honesty is the key. Never cheat anyone, be faithful, give good advice, build relationships, don't be greedy, honesty pays." Patsy Carter Rattigan, "I worked hard, was honest, and I respected my employees. If you are going to succeed you need those qualities." Yvonne Tuttle, "Honesty and integrity always come first. Never underestimate the value of honesty and integrity." Henry Holzkamper, "Honesty prevails. Be proud of what you do, be legitimate and be fair to your customers." Ann Levitan, "Take the high road. Honesty, integrity, and professionalism are the real keys to success." Ron Jedlinski, "do the right thing! Don't lie, cheat, or steal!"

With such a unanimous endorsement for honesty, its value in business and life should be very clear to you. People associate with, and do business with, people they can trust. If you learn nothing more from reading this book than the value of honesty, then you have learned a valuable lesson.

Effort

Entrepreneurs do what they have to do to be successful. Sometimes, long hours, lack of sleep, and personal sacrifice make the difference between success and failure. If you are selling something, get out and make the calls and sooner or later the effort will pay off. Certainly, the harder you work, the luckier you get. It is often said that you create your own luck. You must be willing to do what it takes, be willing to sacrifice your time, comfort, and security to be successful. You must be driven, have tenacity, believe that you can do anything and, you must be a doer. Get it done or get out of the way.

You should be born with a desire to achieve. If you are not highly motivated to achieve, then entrepreneurialism is not for you. Work hard and remember, if you never make a mistake, you are not trying enough things.

Risk Taking

To be an entrepreneur one must be a risk taker. One must be sufficiently committed so that when things are not going well, you have the will to make them go well. As Ron Klein said, "I believe in the philosophy of the turtle, if you don't stick your neck out, you can never get ahead. Be willing to take risks." Patsy Carter Rattigan said, "You must have the drive, the strength, and the willingness to take a risk if you are going to achieve your dreams." And Henry Holzkamper said "Entrepreneurs must be willing to take risks, must have insight into potential opportunities, must have the ability to react to dire circumstances, and the self-confidence to rebound from failure".

If you are not willing to take risks, go work for someone else. But remember, you will never make as much money working for someone as you will when employees work for you. Be willing to fail. Dust yourself off and start again or, find a way to get back on the horse that just threw you.

Vision

Quite often, many people look at the same situation, but few see an opportunity presenting itself. It is the person that can visualize a need and a potential solution or a void in a market or a service that needs to be fulfilled that can become a successful entrepreneur.

Courage

Independence and self-confidence are necessary if someone aspires to be an entrepreneur. You must be decisive! You must have the courage to act! An entrepreneur is a leader by nature. Leaders have no choice but to make decisions. Sure, listen to trusted employees or advisors, but ultimately you must make the decisions. If you vacillate too long you will lose the respect and the confidence of your employees.

Good entrepreneurs have confidence in themselves. They know that failure is not an option. However, in the darkest of times they have the courage to cut the cord and to start anew.

Funding

Entrepreneurs should all learn the term OPM, "Other Peoples Money". Use it! You can do it on your own but if you have investors involved, you have the possibility that you can go back to the well if necessary. As they say, you can start on a shoestring, but it is better to have an emergency fund. Consider having enough capital behind you to last at least a year in hard times.

Employees

Select them carefully. Know that they have the same integrity, drive, and honesty that you have. Consider their actions, their beliefs, and decide whether or not they represent what you want to be. Pay your employees well. They will work harder and there will be less turnover. Turnover is very costly in time lost, training time for the new hire, and recruiting expenses. Offer good benefits and communicate thoroughly and often. Keep an open door to everyone and you won't have a union. Listen to your employees, they often know more about what is going on than you do.

Partnering

Do you need a partner? At some point it is nice to have someone to share the responsibilities. In the early stages of a business you can't get away, but later, if you are going to refresh yourself, you must get away. Having someone you can trust allows you to rest better, knowing that the business is being cared for. Even better, if that person of trust has a vested interest in the success of the business. Always keep more than half of the ownership for yourself. Give your partner or trusted manager the right to disagree with you. If you have a partner or employee that always agrees with you, you don't need him or her.

Professionalism

Dress like a professional. Act like a professional. Be professional. Reports, applications, and communications that you have are read and heard by many people. Even if they have not met you face to face, the accuracy of your paperwork leaves an impression on them. Think about the bank that reviews your loan applications. They judge you by the only thing that they see. If it is sloppy or inaccurate, they may form a negative impression of you.

Listen

Be willing to listen to others. You may not like what they say but you don't need to follow their advice if you don't agree with it. Listen to your mentors first. Express your appreciation for the advice that is offered. It may be worthless, but if you abruptly discard it, the contributor will likely stop offering advice. Learn who to trust.

Vision

Knowing what you want to achieve is half the battle. Entrepreneurs must be creative. They must see opportunities and must be able to visualize how they might capitalize on them.

Finally

An old professor of mine, at Cornell, Dr. Wendel Earle, advised "get out while they will still miss you." A good entrepreneur should be planning for when he or she will walk away and how they will do it.

May your entrepreneurial journey be successful and fulfilling.

Printed in the United States
By Bookmasters